M000251916

WHY COWS NEED COWBOYS

Why Cows Need Cowboys

and Other Seldom-Told Tales from the American West

Edited by Nancy Plain

and Rachelle "Rocky" Gibbons

TWODOT®

Guilford, Connecticut
Helena, Montana

A · TWODOT® · BOOK

An imprint and registered trademark of The Rowman & Littlefield Publishing Group, Inc.
4501 Forbes Blvd., Ste. 200
Lanham, MD 20706
www.rowman.com

Distributed by NATIONAL BOOK NETWORK

Copyright © 2021 by Western Writers of America

All rights reserved. No part of this book may be reproduced in any form or by any electronic or mechanical means, including information storage and retrieval systems, without written permission from the publisher, except by a reviewer who may quote passages in a review.

British Library Cataloguing in Publication Information available

Library of Congress Cataloging-in-Publication Data
Names: Plain, Nancy, editor. | Gibbons, Rachelle, 1956- editor. | Western
 Writers of America.
Title: Why cows need cowboys : and other seldom-told tales from the
 American West / edited by Nancy Plain, and Rachelle "Rocky" Gibbons.
Description: Guilford, Connecticut : TwoDot, [2021] | Includes index. |
 Audience: Ages 13-15 | Audience: Grades 7-9
Identifiers: LCCN 2020055794 (print) | LCCN 2020055795 (ebook) | ISBN
 9781493051076 (paperback) | ISBN 9781493051069 (epub)
Subjects: LCSH: Frontier and pioneer life—West (U.S.)—Juvenile
 literature. | West (U.S.)—Social life and customs—Juvenile literature.
 | Indians of North America—West (U.S.)—Juvenile literature. | West
 (U.S.)—Biography—Juvenile literature.
Classification: LCC F596 .W574 2021 (print) | LCC F596 (ebook) | DDC
 978/.02—dc23
LC record available at https://lccn.loc.gov/2020055794
LC ebook record available at https://lccn.loc.gov/2020055795

This book is dedicated to the founders of Western Writers of America, storytellers all:

Henry Sinclair Drago

Norman Fox

Dwight Newton

Nelson Nye

Wayne Overholser

Tommy Thompson

CONTENTS

INTRODUCTION

We at Western Writers of America (WWA) are delighted to present *Why Cows Need Cowboys and Other Seldom-Told Tales from the American West*, our first anthology for young readers. This collection of twenty nonfiction stories flows naturally from our mission to promote the literature and history of the American West, and we believe that the most compelling part of this mission is educating children about our nation's past. The contributing authors, WWA members all, are experts in their fields and have earned significant literary honors. Among them are winners and finalists in the Spur Award competition, an Owen Wister Award winner, Western Heritage Wrangler Award and Will Rogers Medallion recipients, and winners of numerous other state and national book awards. Many of the writers' works have appeared on bestseller lists and earned starred reviews from prestigious literary publications as well.

But why "seldom-told" tales? Because history is something far more exciting than what students can learn from textbooks alone, and its stories can never all be known. The past was, after all, lived by "ordinary" people, as well as by the bold-faced names. There are riches to be found in the detours and side paths that lie just around the corner from the big events. Davy Crockett fought at the Alamo, but ten-year-old Katie Jennings and eight-year-old Enrique Esparza also played their parts. Theodore Roosevelt accomplished much as one of America's greatest presidents, but how many have heard of his skirmish with the river pirates, who enraged him by stealing his boat? What was it like to be a young Native American hunter in prehistoric times, waiting for a thundering buffalo herd to hurl itself over a cliff? Or to be one of the brave Hotshot firefighters battling the lethal Yarnell Hill Fire of 2013?

From 500 BC to our own twenty-first century, the characters in these pages do extraordinary things. In 1821, a Plains Indian girl treks 1,400 miles to visit the White House. Later in the century, settlers push the frontier ever westward—riding for the Pony Express, driving cattle and driving stagecoaches, and battling the bizarre grasshopper plagues of the 1870s. In the early decades of the twentieth century, a team of daredevil ranching brothers invents modern rodeo. And during World War II, Navajo soldiers, ingeniously using their native language to become "code talkers," play a decisive role in Allied victories. Tales in this anthology range wide in time, topic, and mood, and you'll find here the strange and humorous, the tragic and heroic. However varied their chosen subjects, the writers are united by their love for the American West and its infinite fund of stories.

Founded in 1953, Western Writers of America is the nation's oldest and most distinguished organization of professionals who write about the early frontier and the West. Now, in 2021, as we celebrate our sixty-eighth anniversary, we enjoy a membership of more than seven hundred men and women, spanning the nation from California to Maine and including several countries overseas. WWA is home to internationally renowned authors, as well as to those professionals who are at the beginning of their careers. Our founders were writers of traditional Western fiction, but today WWA comprises not only novelists, but also authors of history and biography, poetry and song, screen and stage plays, children's books, cookbooks, and more. And while in the early years, most of our work was historical in nature, we now embrace contemporary Western writing as much as we cherish works set in the past.

WWA believes that the West embodies a spirit that is uniquely American and that keeping this spirit alive is of paramount importance to the nation and beyond. Our motto is "Literature of the West for the World®."

With *Why Cows Need Cowboys*, we invite young readers to journey westward back in time, to the far past and the not-so-far. For there is a kind of magic in a story well told.

—The Editors, Nancy Plain and Rachelle "Rocky" Gibbons

Why Cows Need Cowboys

Larry Bjornson

Why do cows need cowboys? Well, cows aren't too smart. The smartest cow you'll ever meet can't add two plus two. But they're brainy enough to know they prefer doing what they want rather than what us humans want. So, we need cowboys to persuade them to do things our way.

Let's go back 150 years to South Texas, a time when cows were a lot harder to persuade than today. Imagine you've just been hired for your first real job—you are now a cowboy. And, the boss says he'll pay you three dollars a week, more money than you've ever dreamed of having. Naturally, you'll have to prove yourself to the older cowhands because around here cows run wild and must be caught one by one. Which isn't easy. The Mexicans call this part of Texas the Brasada, the brush country. The Brasada is not like those grassy, wide-open ranches you usually think of. Not at all! It's a thorny, tangled mess with narrow passages and perfect cow hideouts.

And that's why the boss needs another hand.

"Son," the boss had said, "we're puttin' up a herd and takin' 'em nine hundred miles north to Kansas. How'd you like to help?"

Oh, you'd love such a grand adventure, but you ask, "If the cattle are here in Texas, why take them to Kansas? There must be somebody hereabouts that'd want them."

"Sure there is," says the boss. "If you've got the cows, they'll buy 'em all day long."

Ha! you say to yourself, my first day and I'm already smarter than the boss. You'd think he would've thought this through before deciding to take cows on a nine-hundred-mile stroll.

Then the boss says, "Now, son, whaddya think a Texan that buys them cows is gonna do with 'em?"

That surely has you stumped. "I don't think I know, sir."

"He's gonna drive 'em nine hundred miles north to Kansas, that's what."

"Huh! But why?"

"Because when you sell a cow in Texas, you get three or four dollars. But sell that cow in Kansas, you get thirty or forty dollars."

This stereo card (early 3-D photo) shows a horse and cowboy holding a lassoed cow. COURTESY NATIONAL COWBOY & WESTERN HERITAGE MUSEUM'S DONALD C. & ELIZABETH M. DICKINSON RESEARCH CENTER, THROWN! COWBOY AND HORSE HOLDING A LASSOED COW, KANSAS, CIRCA 1920. KEYSTONE VIEW COMPANY 2004.074

Now you feel kinda dumb, but another question hits you.

"So, if you've got a cow here, and then you got that same cow there, in Kansas, how come some Kansas fool pays you so much more for it?"

The boss gives you a pitying look. "Because Kansas has fewer cattle and more railroads than Texas. And they use their railroads to carry our cattle to the big stockyard towns like Kansas City and Chicago. And from there, other railroads take the beef to all the cities in the East. More hungry people than you can imagine."

It seems the boss is smarter than you thought.

"Just one problem," says the boss.

"Uh-huh."

"I don't have any cattle."

"Ohhhh."

"But I know where they are."

"Ahhhh!"

"And I want you to go get 'em."

"How many?"

"Oh, two thousand, give or take."

You study the boss's face to see if he's kidding, but he looks about as funny as a rope burn.

"Son, here's how we're gonna work it. Some nearby ranchers are bringin' in smaller bunches. So, we don't have to catch the whole two thousand. We'll join 'em all up into one big herd, and when we get to Kansas, we'll sell the lot of 'em and then bring back everybody's share of money."

"Uh-huh."

"Is that all you got to say, son? You aren't a dolt, are you? I can't abide a dolt."

"No, sir! I was wondering about your cattle."

"Ah, my cattle! Well, we're gonna catch my cattle—me and you and six of my other hands. We'll snatch, say, eight hundred. I've seen you rope and ride. You're pretty good, and by the time we're done, you'll be a whole lot better."

The boss must've decided you looked too bright and breezy. He puts a hand on your shoulder, and giving you a look that's both hard and concerned, he says, "Don't get yourself killed."

Fact is, proud as you are to make three dollars a week, this job for sure isn't the safest thing a fellow can do. If you were to ask the boss why he hired you, he'd likely answer that one of his cowhands quit. That might mean a cowhand quit, but it's probably the boss's short way of saying that one of his men got an arm broke, or a rib busted, or got otherwise "stove up," meaning too badly hurt to keep working.

You see, this is the brush country, and nothing out here likes you.

The horses don't like you. Most of them were wild once, and they haven't forgotten how much they liked freedom. Memories like that make them cranky. So, if they see a chance, they'll kick your head off, or bite a chunk out of you, or stomp your chest when you're down. And any time you're in the saddle, they might just decide to buck you off. They're both your partner and your enemy. There's only two good things about them—they hate letting a cow escape, and they love the chase. Turns out, horses believe hunting cows is a game, and just like us humans, they want to win.

The cows dislike you even more than the horses. They're just hateful. Why? Because they know you've come to capture them. Now, just so you understand, these cows aren't like regular cows, all fat and sleepy with little bitty horns. These longhorn cows are seven hundred to one thousand pounds of pure wildness. They're fast, corded with muscle, and each of their horns can be as long as a tall man's leg.

Even the land doesn't like you. Here and there you'll find dusty natural clearings, but mostly the Brasada is a choking snarl of cactus, scrub underbrush, skeletal bushes, and low stalky trees, all of it crowded and twisted into a huge, thorny, scraggy confusion. Everything that grows bristles with spines, sawtooth edges, and rough surfaces. And winding through this withered jungle run pinched little paths beaten in by the passage of wary longhorns venturing from their hideouts.

It's not a place you'd ride through as fast as your horse can run. But that's what you're going to do. Starting tomorrow.

You might ask, why would anyone want such a job? Easy—it's exciting! And people around here admire anyone tough and skilled enough to do it.

You'll stay in camp during this cow hunt. That evening, after supper, the men gather around the fire, leaning back on their saddles, some squatting, balanced on their toes, telling stories, joshing, and laughing. No one pays any attention to you. Once, you make a little joke, trying to be part of it all, but they only glance at you, and no one laughs. It's not that they dislike you. It's just that you're an outsider until you prove yourself.

Bright and early the next morning, you start your first workday. Actually, not so bright, since the sun is still snoozing below the horizon when you crawl out of your blankets. But you don't care. You're too excited, and kinda scared. The boss's words about not getting killed are still in your head.

The boss has given you a string of sixteen horses. That's a lot. Cowhands working on a grassy prairie might be assigned only eight. But here in the Brasada, horses work hard and get stiff and sore and weary, and you can use one up mighty fast. So, you need plenty of fresh mounts.

While you're working for the boss, the horses in your string are yours alone. No one else can ride them without your permission. On the other hand, there's probably horses in your string no one wants to ride anyway. Every string has its jug-headed, kickers, biters, and back-fallers. Mean enough that the thought of riding one might make you toss up your breakfast.

You're fitted out with mostly hand-me-down brush gear and clothes. But it's all still useable, and because it's old, it doesn't make you look like more of a greenhorn than you are.

Most important is an old hull of a saddle, so worn that parts of its wooden tree, the saddle's skeleton, peek through the leather here and there. Some saddles have one cinch, the strap that wraps under the horse, but brush country saddles like yours are double-rigged, having two cinches to make certain the saddle doesn't rotate or fly off when you're roping wild cattle.

You have a sweat-stained Stetson hat. The brim, though, isn't as wide as most cowboy hats. Big brim hats just get torn off in the brush. Your hat's brim is also rolled to a point in front.

You've got Star-brand boots with two-inch heels and big, round, nickel-plated spurs out back that ring when you walk. A heavy, tattered, waist-length denim brush jacket. Thick gloves with long cuffs. A pair of scuffed, tough-as-nails, bull-hide leggings that cover your legs and buckle at the waist. Around your neck hangs a big red bandana handkerchief, good for everything from wiping sweat to tying a cow's legs together.

And, you have a braided rawhide rope. Most cowboys use ropes made of fiber, but in the brush country, a rawhide rope is best because it's heavier. It's a joy to use, able to slam through thin brush that would tangle a lighter fiber rope. You can throw a loop flashing through the air with marvelous accuracy—if it misses, it's probably your fault.

After breakfast, the horse wrangler brings in the horses, and each man calls for the one he wants roped out. Of course, you're new and don't know much about your mounts yet. So, when you call for a certain star-faced sorrel, you hear the men groan and snicker, and you know you've picked an outlaw. And sure enough, you had to be on guard every second while saddling to avoid being bit or kicked. After a few failed tries, you blindfolded that churn head with your bandana, and he quieted enough to let you lace on the saddle.

But when you climbed on and jerked off the blind, the horse humped its back, threw its head down, and then shot straight up into the air. After that, there was quite a spell of bucking and bellering, hooves slamming, spurs ringing, and cowboys cheering, but you stayed in the saddle until finally the horse broke into a trot, and it was over. You heard one of the men declare, "But say, can't that kid ride!" and you knew you were a little closer to being a part of them.

An hour later, you and your horse are deep in a thorny maze of mesquite, black chaparral, prickly pear, Spanish dagger, devil's head, and rat tail cactus. One of the men rides up and says, "A little advice, kid. When you're hot after some cow, hittin' the brush, don't ever close your eyes. You'll want to, more than anything, but don't do it."

Just then, three of the boss's catch dogs trot past. They go on down a ways, and suddenly the lead dog lets out a piercing yelp and sprints into a dense thicket. The other dogs follow, baying and barking. There's a crashing and popping of brittle brush, and two longhorns explode from the thicket and race down a narrow, winding path with the dogs on their heels.

Your horse lunges after them so quickly you nearly tumble off backward. The other cowhand is behind you at first, but when the two cows split up, he veers down a different path and disappears. Now you're alone. The brush is flying at you faster than you can think, head on, high and low, left and right. You dodge it all as best you can, throwing yourself down one side of the horse, lying flat atop, down the other side, always trying to anticipate the horse's next move so you can keep your balance.

It's up to you to stay in the saddle. The horse doesn't watch out for you. He is totally focused on catching the fleeing longhorn. Streaking along, he dives through holes and gaps in the brush, scrapes under arching mesquite trunks, leaps low limbs, and slams through higher ones. He throws his weight this way and that. His body twists in midair. He does not take you into account. Branches crack, hooves rattle against the earth, dust flies, thorny brush rakes and whips at you. It's up to you—get out of the way or fling up a protective arm or shoulder or leg and take the hit.

And then, it's all too much. You close your eyes. Just for an instant. But when you open them, an unbreakable branch hits you square in the chest, and next you know, you're on your back in the dirt. Your horse is gone. The cow you were chasing is gone. The catch dogs are baying in the far distance.

With a groan, you stand up and start walking. After a while, the rider you started out with comes along leading your horse. He grins and hands off your reins.

"Kid, when you're workin' cows, you gotta stick closer to your horse."

"I closed my eyes," you say.

"You ain't the first."

"Never even got my rope out."

"Kid, don't go feelin' sorry for yourself. Plenty more chances to get it right."

And there were.

Within the hour, you are again racing through the brush, closing fast on a dodging, swerving longhorn. You have your rope in hand, but the limbs and branches flashing past cut in too close to allow throwing a clean loop. You'll have to wait for an opening and hope you don't lose your cow first.

As you expect, a clearing opens up briefly. At once you whirl out a small, tight loop, whipped to terrific speed, and hand, arm, and shoulder all work together to fire the loop like a rawhide bullet at the cow's bounding legs.

The loop sings through the air and slaps around the cow's rear hooves just as they rise from the ground. As you tie off the rope to the saddle horn, your horse sits down, front legs bracing, and an instant later the cow comes to the end of the rope with a wrenching shock and falls plowing into the ground.

You just caught your first brush country longhorn. You feel proud. In a couple of weeks, you'll be a first-class cow persuader.

The Last Drop:
From Death to Life at Madison Buffalo Jump

Matthew P. Mayo

It is 500 BC, and tribes come together for their annual bison drive, a shared celebration of rebirth and replenishment. After weeks of preparation and waiting, scouts spot a herd nearby, and the hunt is on. Among the warriors, a boy participating for the first time is chosen to wear a bison calfskin and lead the grazing herd toward the clifftop. Soon the massive animals are funneled toward the drop-off by waving warriors amid rock cairns.

At the base of the cliffs, a girl joins the women for the first time in butchering the fallen beasts. They render the bison into meat, pemmican, bone tools, vessels, garments, tipi coverings, and more. It has been a good drive and the tribes give thanks, knowing they will survive another year.

◆◆◆

He had not expected the choking clouds of dry grit and powdered dung that filled his nostrils, caked his eyes, and peppered his tongue and teeth. He clenched them tighter and continued his hunched-over walk, one foot poised, then the next, then pause to shake his head and bellow, to mimic the bison calf he had become in order to lead this herd to the far cliff's edge, to lead the herd to its death.

Droplets of sweat stung his eyes and he squeezed them together quickly to help clear his vision. He swung around once more and stared at the lead bison. Large brown eyes, rimmed with yellow and caked with flies and red with bloodlines, stared back. They were set in a thick head as wide as the boy's outstretched arms, and nearly as tall as he stood.

The brute snorted and lowered its mighty head, then shook it slowly back and forth, back and forth. Flies and dust boiled up, then settled.

The boy sensed the bull was becoming angry—the big males were always angry. The boy knew if he did not move, he was the first thing that would be stomped and trampled and pounded into

Herd of bison on the upper Missouri LIBRARY OF CONGRESS PRINTS AND PHOTOGRAPHS DIVISION

the dust of the dry earth by that big, wide, hairy head. But why? Had he not imitated the calf as he had practiced? Yes, but the beast still seemed suspicious.

A breeze pushed forward from the rear of the herd, carrying with it more dust. But it would also disguise any scents from his tribesmen that might arouse suspicion in the bison. The boy coughed and did his best to pinch off a sneeze building in his nose.

He was but twenty paces ahead of the lead bull, far enough that with the animal's poor eyesight it would still think him a bison calf. In truth, he was a young warrior wearing the skin of a calf. It was his task, the most important of the day, to tease the leaders of the herd into following him, and it was working.

The lead bison walked faster, and the following herd of thirty beasts did the same, their hooves thudding in a slow, mismatched, drumming rhythm.

Ahead he saw the beginnings of the drive lane, fifty paces across at the mouth, marked with cairns, rocks stacked in piles at intervals. There were also logs and great tufts of grasses twisted together, anything his people could find to define the sides of the lane. Most of these had been placed there by their forebears many hunts ago. Though current tribes, too, had repaired and added to the angling lines of cairns and logs over past days.

It was in this narrowing lane he would run, leading the herd to the cliff. He must not fail, or his own tribe, as well as the three others who had joined them for the hunt, would all know great hunger in the coming cold season. There would be no food for the growling bellies of the babies and old ones, no sinews for lashing, no pemmican, no skins for wearing, no blankets for warmth, no bone tools . . .

The boy shook his head to dispel the treacherous, doubting thoughts and squinted. Far ahead he saw what might be the edge of the cliff. It seemed to blend with the distant vista, though the morning sun's brightness and the boiling clouds of dust conspired to blur the scene.

Behind him he heard the bison thunder forward, stiff legged but gaining speed. That could only mean that the runners and hunters were closing together, driving them from the rear of the herd.

Move! Run faster! Isn't that what Grandfather had taught him? Keep ahead of the herd, not only to lead them to the cliff's edge, but to stay alive. Alive, yes, that was the word. The boy gulped hard, swallowing back a mouthful of grit and dust and powdered dung and blinked his eyes.

Urged on by the other hunters, some capering beneath wolf skins at the rear of the herd, the great shaggy beasts broke into a run. Keeping low, lest they discover his ruse and shy from him, the boy dashed ahead.

But the great shaggy beasts gained on him. He felt hot breaths from that mammoth, red-eyed bull steaming the back of his neck. The lane narrowed as they ran, and now he was uncertain where the cliff's edge lay. Yet he ran, crouched low and not daring to look back lest he lose his footing and stumble. Then they would be on him, pounding him into the earth even as they thundered forward to their own deaths.

Through sweat-filled eyes, he saw men leap from their hiding spots behind the rock cairns and logs, their arms wide and waving. They held aloft their spears, their atlatls, and clubs, and their harsh shouts echoed loud with meaning. Others closed in, chasing from the rear, prodding and shouting and howling fearful, savage cries.

They drove back into the great running mass of animals the beasts that had strayed close to the edges of the drivelines, lest they break from the group and scatter the herd. Such escape would ruin the drives forever, for bison have long memories. Then all would be lost, and the people would starve in the coming seasons.

Unbidden, and at the wrong moment—for Grandfather had told him he must not think of anything save for being a calf, and especially not when the cliff's edge loomed so close—she was in his mind. The girl. Right now, far below, she would be there with the other women. This was a girl he had seen for two hunts now, far across the vast campsite, she of another tribe.

"Boy, are you listening to me?"

The boy had blinked hard twice and saw once more nothing but his own breath feathering white before him in the dark of the early morning. "Yes, Grandfather."

"Good, because I thought perhaps your mind was filled with thoughts of a young woman."

Too fast, the boy spun, his eyes wide and shining, to see Grandfather's smiling face staring back at him. "Do not think you are the first to feel as you do, boy."

But now it was all dust and the girl and the heavy, rasping breaths of the ragged bison running close, too close behind him, and he could not run any faster and he was petrified of stumbling, even though he felt every sharp edge of rock and prickly plant through his moccasin soles as he gasped for breath, dusty, dung-smelling breath, the rank stink of the flopping, half-cured calfskin tied about his neck and chest and arms and belly. No time for the girl! And yet, she would not leave his mind alone . . .

It had been at last year's drive they had spoken to each other, however fleetingly. She had commented on his grandfather, a legend among the tribes. He had grunted and nodded. Fool! Even now, the boy felt his face and ears heat deeply at the memory.

He had been but a child then, not allowed to participate with the men, and had been told to assist the women with the butchering. The memory of it shamed him still. To think she had seen him in such a lowly position.

He knew she'd only been showing him a kindness she would any little boy. But not this year. This year she would see him for what he was, the lead runner, the only warrior selected for the honor.

The boy recalled the vast encampment where the four tribes had staked their spots, the same as each year. In his mind he saw the sea of tipis, anchored at their bases with rings of stone, saw smoke rising from the fire pits, saw camp dogs and children at play. By the time the drive began, the women would have assumed their positions and kindled the fires and honed their fleshing tools—bone scrapers and stone knives—that would serve to render meat from bone.

What meat not eaten fresh tonight during the grand feast would be sliced thin and dried on racks for the coming winter. Some would be pounded and mashed with fat and berries to make toothsome pemmican.

The girl would be there with the other women, awaiting the bison to hurl themselves off the edge, bellowing and bleating and screaming, their big eyes white in fear and anger and, finally, in surrender as they fell from the sky at the women's feet. And all because he had made it so.

Yes, she would be there. With her laughing eyes and serious mouth, with her long hair that shone darker than the wing of any raven yet born. She would see him high above, atop the cliff, dropping nimbly from the edge to the narrow precipice where he would prance like a goat even as the mighty bison leaders dropped and slammed and tumbled and rolled past him to the bottom, so far down, piling their wrecked bodies, all because of him! He would feed the people.

Even in his aching lungs and dulled, wooden legs and sweat-stinging eyes, the boy smiled a grim smile over tight-set teeth and thought of the glory and of the girl awaiting him. And then he jumped off the cliff's edge.

⚊ ⚊

Far below, the girl held a nut-brown hand to her eyes and stood in a long row with the other women, squinting up at the ragged edge of the cliff far above. "There!" shouted an old one. All the women glanced briefly her way, then followed the elder's pointing finger toward a thin feather of dust. As they watched, it bloomed over the cliff, billowing and spreading like a storm cloud.

"Soon," whispered the girl's mother, and silence settled over them once more. Far behind at the tipis, they heard a child wailing, then that, too, ceased, as if the baby had also sensed what was about to happen.

The girl shifted her weight to her other foot and licked her lips. There was one thing she wanted to see, even more than the sadly promising sight of the great black and brown animals tumbling from the cliff's edge. She wished to see the boy, ahead of the herd, disguised under the calfskin. It was his first time as the lead runner, teasing the bulls forward, and she had never known such worry.

She heard them now, a distant *thud thud thud* that grew louder with each moment. Soon they would see the herd. But first they must see the boy in the lead. They must watch him dart to the side and drop off the edge onto the narrow ledge. There he must make himself small and tight, hugging the rock face lest the falling, flailing beasts collide with him and knock him far below onto the graveled slope, a false bison crushed and broken among the true bison.

Then the girl knew she could not bear it if the boy were killed.

It would be an honorable way to die, to be sure. There would be songs sung of him, and storytelling around the great fires. For many of his tribe, there would be much lamentation and displays of grief, but the girl did not want that. She wanted him to live because they were to be wife and husband. Though this was the first time she had thought of this, she knew it would be so. Somehow, she was sure of it.

The rumbling grew louder, drew closer, the dust cloud boiled greater, rising and blotting out the blue of the sky. The jamming, pounding, thudding of hooves, separate sounds but moments before, now became one huge sound she felt in her fingertips. It pulsed in her ears, then deeper, deeper inside her until her chest filled with the sound.

With no warning, black shapes burst from the center of the great cloud of dust, just before the cliff's edge. The girl's gut tightened—they should stop! Don't they know they will die? But the bison knew only their frantic fear, and they thundered onward, ever closer to the edge. Where was the boy?

The girl held her breath, shielded with both hands above her eyes as if to dispel the dust and distance. She scarcely felt her mother's arm close tight about her, her firm hand squeezing her daughter's shoulder.

The girl trembled and held her breath and watched. Where was the boy? Could that first dark shape she saw have been him? But hadn't that shape plunged off the edge, the first of the many to do so? Surely a young warrior might survive a thirty-foot drop.

She wanted to ask her mother, wanted to hear someone tell her yes, he was fine. But the sounds from the cliff bloomed louder, and the sight, though something she'd seen many times before, today overwhelmed her.

It seemed never to end, as the big bodies of the bison flailed and tumbled, colliding with each other at the edge, then in the air, before dropping atop one another at the base of the slope.

She heard great slapping sounds as they slammed into each other. She heard bones snap, heard the beasts scream in their raw, confused terror. Dozens of them bellowing in surprise, then screaming in raw fear, trembling, white foam and blood gouting from their mouths in their sudden, unendurable pain. Pain that would only be quelled by the thrusts of many spears, ending in a slow, agonized death.

"There!"

It was her mother, shouting beside her ear and pointing, her face close to the girl's. "You see? You see him?"

And suddenly the girl did see, she saw the boy just where he should be, pressed close to the cliff's face, tight to the far side of the tiny ledge onto which he had to leap at the very last of moments. She knew then he was alive and looking down at her, too, and she could not help smiling.

Her mother's reassuring, firm hand squeezed her shoulder once more. "Come, now we do our part."

The girl nodded and could not conceal the smile on her face. Nor could her mother.

With the other women, they spread out and worked their way up the slopes, proceeding with caution among the still-thrashing beasts, drawing their stone blades across the throats of those not yet dead, slitting open the great, hairy bellies to begin the day's long labors.

The work was foul. The blood steamed and thickened in the heat. Sluggish flies bulged with it, winging slow and annoying as they fed. The girl had tied her long black hair behind her head with a leather thong, but still strands slipped loose and danced in her eyes. She blew them away and tried to think of something more pleasant. Which meant thinking about anything else.

This was her first drive participating as one of the women. She'd been given her own stone knife, and the young ones in her charge waited for her to tell them what to do with the flesh she freed from the bones, how to pull hard on the great beast's blood-slick hide, peeling it back, then rolling it upon itself before setting it aside. Later it would be cleaned, scraped, stretched, dried, and softened.

There was pride in this work, and though she was tired and the day not half through, and though the autumn sun felt nearly as hot as it had a season before, there was no river close by for lazy bathing. Now was the time for work. For this annual bison drive had been a plentiful hunt, with many bodies of the mighty animals before them, still waiting to be butchered.

This was the time of year when her tribe members came together with those of other tribes. The people relied on this hunt for so much. Not only for food, but for their tipis, which were covered with bison hides, and for their dresses and trousers and shirts and moccasins, all fashioned from the skins. The animals' tendons, or sinews, when stretched and scraped and smoothed, were the thread that bound together vessels of skin and gut used to carry water and fire. Sinew formed the seams of their clothing and secured the harnesses used on the dogs to drag goods from camp to camp.

The girl did her best to forget the sight of the skin-clad youth on the ledge of the cliff above, but she could not quite forget, for he was a bison runner. Thoughts of him renewed the rare smile on her mouth.

She did not look up again, for he would no longer be on the ledge. He would now be among the rest of the men, spearing the last of the struggling bison.

Perhaps tonight at the feast, after they gave thanks to the gods for their good fortune and great bounty, the boy would dance before her, enacting his brave and successful hunt on this special day, a day when everyone helped to feed the tribes for another year.

HAYNE-HUDJIHINI
THE EAGLE OF DELIGHT.

PUBLISHED BY F. W. GREENOUGH, PHILAD.ª
Drawn Printed & Coloured at I.T.Bowens Lithographic Establishment Nº 94 Walnut St.
Entered according to act of Congress in the Year 1838 by F. Greenough, in the Clerks Office of the District Court of the Eastern District of Penn.ª

Hayne Hudjihini, the Eagle of Delight LIBRARY OF CONGRESS PRINTS AND PHOTOGRAPHS DIVISION, PHILAD[ELPHI]A: PUBLISHED BY F.W. GREENOUGH, C1838.

Eagle of Delight:
The Plains Indian Girl in the White House

Jean A. Lukesh

Eagle of Delight wore her long black hair parted in the middle and braided behind her ears. Sometimes she painted a red mineral called vermillion, or cinnabar, along that part in her hair. Red was a sacred color for her people, the Otoe (Oh-toe) Indians. Eagle of Delight's ears were pierced in many places, too, and she wore several beaded hoop earrings. And on her forehead, right between her dark brown eyes, she had a tiny, pale blue tattoo, showing that she was a very special person. When she was born, at her family's earth-lodge village, sometime around 1806, she was called "Beloved Child."

That was about the time that the explorers Meriwether Lewis and William Clark visited her Otoe-Missouri homeland. It was near the broad, flat rivers known as the Platte, the Elkhorn, and the Missouri, in what is now northeastern Nebraska. Eagle of Delight and her family would never have guessed that someday she—as just a teenager—would make a journey back East to the homeland of Lewis and Clark, where she would become famous and greatly admired.

During her childhood years, Eagle of Delight ran races and played tag with her friends. She rode horses and mothered homemade dolls made of cornhusks. She listened to the stories of her people and learned about life, just as other Plains Indian children did. When she was older, she became known as *Hayne Hudjihini* (Hay-nuh Hoo-djuh-hee-nee) in her native language. Her new name may have meant "Eagle of Delight," a name showing that she was loved.

Her parents were important members of their tribe, and Eagle was taught to honor, respect, and be kind to others, no matter their age or position in the tribe. She was expected to do only good things: no lying, no name-calling, and no hurting or making fun of others. From special elders of her tribe, she received teachings about the ways of her people. When the elders felt she was ready, she became a member of the highly regarded Night Dance Society. Before long, she would prove to be a great role model for her people and an inspiration to others as well.

To show that she was a member of the Night Dancers, Eagle of Delight received the tattoo between her eyes during a special ceremony, when she was about thirteen. That tattoo was a high honor among her people. She may have received it in 1819 or 1820, the same year that other explorers and military men—including Major Stephen Long, his soldiers, scientists, reporters, and an Indian agent named Benjamin O'Fallon, who was also William Clark's nephew—came to meet with the Otoe-Missouri chiefs and their people.

These explorers took special note of the second chief, or half-chief, of the Otoe, a man known as Prairie Wolf. They said he was "brave, strong, and intelligent" and also "tall, muscular, and stern, but good-natured, with a good sense of humor." They called him "one of the most brave and generous warriors of the Missouri Valley."

Like some other Plains Indians, the Otoe people raised corn and hunted buffalo and other wild game for their food. Blizzards froze the land in winter, and the sun baked it dry in summer. Life was difficult on the plains. People there did not live long in those days, so they often married early.

By the time Eagle of Delight was fifteen, she was married to the half-chief Prairie Wolf. Her husband had many names, including *Iotan* (I-oh-tan), *Yutan* (Yu-tan), and *Shaumonekusse* (Sha-mon-uh-koo-see). He was a well-respected chief and a good provider for his family—including all five of his wives. To show that he was a mighty hunter, he often wore a string of bear claws around his neck and a headdress decorated with a set of buffalo horns and red-dyed horsehair. He was older than Eagle of Delight, but people said he treated her well and respected her. In turn, she seemed to be happy with him.

Eagle of Delight and Prairie Wolf had not been married long when the Indian Agent Benjamin O'Fallon returned, this time to invite chiefs from a few different Plains Indian tribes to join him on a long journey. Together, chiefs of the Pawnee, Omaha, Otoe-Missouri, and Kansa tribes would be the first official Plains Indian delegation—sixteen men in all—to visit the East. In 1821, they would travel about 1,400 miles one way, first going down the "Muddy Missouri River" to meet William Clark in St. Louis, then head northeast to visit the president of the United States in Washington City (now called Washington, DC). And several months later, they would travel home the same way.

Prairie Wolf was one of two Otoe chiefs chosen to make that journey along with the other Plains Indian leaders. Eagle of Delight must have felt proud and honored that her husband was one of the chosen delegates. But she was also probably afraid that something bad might happen to him while he was away. He could be hurt or killed. She might never see him again.

She did not have to worry for long. Prairie Wolf refused to make the journey without his new and favorite wife, Eagle of Delight. So, it was soon decided that she would go with her husband, the other chiefs, and Agent O'Fallon and his men. She would be the first woman to go east with a Native American delegation.

The trip by horse, wagon, boat, and carriage was long, strange, and difficult for the Plains Indians, especially for the only woman. For the first time in their lives, the delegates stayed in houses and hotels, sat at tables, and used silverware to eat. They also slept in beds instead of on fur robes on the ground. Eagle of Delight had no other women to talk to, but she seemed to get along well. She knew she was not really a delegate like the chiefs, but she always did her best to represent her family and her people. She never complained or did anything to dishonor her husband.

When the delegates reached Washington City, newspapers reported their story and made them famous. They became very popular, especially Eagle of Delight, her husband, and a young Pawnee chief. Crowds of people formed to meet "the Western Indians" in their feather headdresses, leather clothing, and moccasins, and to follow them down the streets wherever they went. In addition to Washington City, the Indians also toured Philadelphia, New York, and other big cities of the East. The Indian delegates were amazed by the tall buildings and the large numbers of people and carriages in the towns.

The Indians visited many important people in schools and private homes. They toured grand buildings and went to parties. They even attended a dance at the White House, where they met President James Monroe, congressmen, and foreign ambassadors and their wives. One well-dressed gentleman asked Eagle of Delight to dance with him, but she turned him down. She felt it would be improper to dance with a man who was not her husband.

The chiefs and Eagle of Delight met President Monroe at least three times in the White House. There all the men gave and received gifts and made speeches. The head chiefs of each of the tribes also received peace medals from the president.

When the speeches and gift giving were over, President Monroe asked Eagle of Delight if she would like to make a speech, too, just as the men had done. At first, she said no, thinking that it was not her place. After all, she was not a delegate. But while the president encouraged her to talk, some of the chiefs started laughing at the idea of a woman speaking in council. At that point, Eagle of Delight knew exactly what she wanted to say.

In her unprepared speech and speaking through an interpreter, she said something like this: "President Monroe, just now you gave peace medals to the main chiefs of our tribes. But you did not give medals to the half-chiefs like my husband and the other young men. Perhaps you should also give peace medals to these half-chiefs now, to remind them of this friendship. For in the future, these half-chiefs might all be head chiefs."

The president was surprised and delighted by Eagle of Delight's speech and also by her intelligence and diplomacy. The minor chiefs were pleased by her idea too. Since the peace medals came in three different sizes, President Monroe quickly called for one of his men to bring each of the minor chiefs a smaller medal. That made everyone happy.

Then Monroe asked Eagle of Delight what other gift she might like to have from him in place of a peace medal. She smiled and through her interpreter said, "I would really like a red dress—one like the dresses that the women of the East wear—to go with the green pantaloons [pant-like leggings] that I have already received as a gift from you."

President Monroe smiled and sent someone to find a red dress for her. Before long, Eagle of Delight received an orange-red dress decorated with tiny gold flowers, along with a white fur jacket. She was delighted with the dress and jacket and wore them often during her time in the East. During that visit, her personality and good manners won her the nickname "the Darling of Washington Society." She had definitely earned her place as a delegate alongside her husband and the other chiefs.

Whether in their own native dress or in the formal clothing given to them as gifts, Eagle of Delight and her husband, Prairie Wolf, often visited their new friends while in the East. Some of their favorites were a doctor and his family. Eagle of Delight loved to play with the family's children and to hold and feed their baby. She spoke almost no English, but her husband was very interested in learning as much of the language as he could. He memorized words and phrases and translated conversations to and from his wife.

Prairie Wolf had a great sense of humor too. Once while he and Eagle of Delight were visiting their doctor friend in his medical office, they noticed a complete human skeleton hanging from a wire. At first the Native Americans were shocked and a bit frightened, but the doctor quickly explained that he used the skeleton to show his patients how bones worked and how broken bones could be mended.

Prairie Wolf understood. He nodded his head and smiled, and then he made a joke: In his formal coat and tall hat, he stepped forward and gently shook the skeleton's hand. At the same time, he spoke very politely in his best English, saying, "How do you do?" Everyone in the house enjoyed the joke. Eagle of Delight smiled. She was very proud of her husband.

In February 1822, all seventeen of the delegates may have had their portraits painted by a young artist named Charles Bird King. Some of those portraits were copied by hand several times. The paintings were then displayed in many places in Washington City, even in storefronts and in the Smithsonian Castle building.

Eagle of Delight's portrait showed her wearing the red dress and white fur jacket that President Monroe had given her. Her portrait and the portrait of the young Pawnee chief became the two most popular paintings. They were copied the most often and were displayed with paintings of her husband and others from the delegation. Two groups of five paintings each were even sent a few years later to Denmark and the Netherlands.

In early spring of 1822, it was time for the delegates to go home. Copies of their portraits and many other gifts were loaded into several wagons. Then the delegates climbed into carriages to leave Washington City. They would all make the long journey back home to their own villages. But shortly after returning home, Eagle of Delight probably died of measles, an illness she had contracted near the end of her journey. Even though he had four other wives, her husband was heartbroken, and he mourned a long time for her. In time he would become head chief of the Otoe people.

The delegates had gone home, but they would not be completely forgotten back East. In the early 1830s, more hand-colored copies of their portraits were created in lithographs or woodcut printings. Some of these artworks were selected for the *McKenney-Hall Indian Gallery* book, a new three-volume set of over 120 portraits of Native American visitors to the East. The portrait of Eagle of Delight, in her red dress and white jacket, was one of eight paintings of Native American women included in the set.

In 1961, another president was in office in the White House. His name was John F. Kennedy. When he and his wife—First Lady Jacqueline "Jackie" Kennedy—first moved into the White House, they noticed that the furniture and decorations inside were in bad condition. Mrs. Kennedy then made it her mission to redecorate the interior of the mansion with things that might have had a place there in its long history.

A man named Vincent Price was chairman of the committee that Mrs. Kennedy had formed to find just the right items for the inside of the White House. Price was best known as a movie star who acted in many horror films, including *The Fly* and *The House on Haunted Hill*, but he was also an artist and a well-known art critic. In 1962, he located a set of five portraits of the Native American delegates who had visited the White House during the 1821 to 1822 tour. One of those portraits was of Eagle of Delight. Another one of the paintings was of her husband, Prairie Wolf, and a third one depicted the famous young Pawnee chief.

When Vincent Price found the set of five paintings, they were being offered for sale in the Netherlands. He made a deal that enabled the employees of Sears, Roebuck and Company to buy the portraits for forty thousand dollars and to give them to Mrs. Kennedy in the White House. That was 140 years after Eagle of Delight and her fellow delegates had visited President James Monroe and his wife in that very same building.

Mrs. Kennedy accepted the portraits on behalf of herself, the White House, and the American people. They are now generally kept on permanent display in the library room of the White House. Sometimes they can also be seen in books, movies, and documentary films.

Although just a teen during that long-ago visit, Eagle of Delight had proven herself to be a diplomat, a delegate, a representative, and a "First Lady" of her people. She, her husband, and their three other portrait companions would be proud of their place in the White House today—and of their placement there by one of America's most beloved first ladies, Jackie Kennedy.

Enrique Esparza Remembered the Alamo

William Groneman III

February 23, 1836, could not have been more exciting and in many ways more frightening for young Enrique Esparza. A force of Texan revolutionaries had been occupying his town of San Antonio de Béxar since the previous December, when they had driven out the Mexican Army under General Martin Perfecto de Cos. The Texans had battled from house to house in town, forcing the Mexican soldiers into the old Spanish mission across the San Antonio River. With no help coming and no chance of victory, Cos had surrendered. The Texans released him and his men to return to the interior of Mexico on parole, never to take up arms against Texas again. Today Enrique and his family were crossing the river to join the revolutionaries in that same mission, known as the Alamo, because the Mexican Army had returned.

Texas, part of the larger Mexican state of Coahuila y Téjas, wanted independence from the heavy-handed leadership of President Antonio Lopez de Santa Anna. Originally its residents had sought separate statehood within the Mexican Federation, but once the fighting began, independence remained their only path.

Things had quieted down since the fighting in December 1835. The Texan force, under Lieutenant Colonel James C. Neill, was occupying fortifications in the town itself and in the old mission. The citizens of San Antonio had become accustomed to their presence. But as time went on, the Texan force was dwindling, along with its supplies and money. Soon Neill had not enough men to defend both the town and mission. He dispatched couriers calling for assistance and reinforcements since he knew San Antonio to be the key to the control of Texas, and he knew the Mexican Army would return.

By February, no help had come. So, Neill gave temporary command of his post to Lieutenant Colonel William Barret Travis while he ventured out himself to obtain reinforcements and supplies. (Travis would ultimately share command with Colonel James Bowie.)

Enrique Esparza's father, Gregorio, had fought against the Mexican soldiers in December and helped drive them out of Texas. Now Gregorio worried about his wife, Ana, their three

This stereo card shows the exterior of the Alamo in San Antonio, Texas. LIBRARY OF CONGRESS PRINTS AND PHOTO-GRAPHS DIVISION, COPYRIGHT, 1909, BY STEREO-TRAVEL CO. NO. 59.

sons—Enrique, Francisco, and Manuel—and Ana's ten-year-old daughter, Maria. He had received word of the Mexican Army's approach in early 1836 and was waiting for a promised wagon to move his family to safety in San Felipe. But the wagon never came. On February 23, Gregorio's friend John W. Smith, godfather to Enrique's youngest brother Manuel, warned the family of the enemies' expected arrival. Smith advised Gregorio that all who were friends to the Americans had better take refuge with them in the Alamo. The Esparzas took his advice and that day made many trips back and forth, moving possessions from their home to the fort.

Young Enrique remembered entering the Alamo, a large, open area of almost three acres enclosed by walls and buildings, with a church being the largest. "We went into the church portion. It was shut up when we arrived. We were admitted through a small window. I distinctly remember that I climbed through the window and over a cannon that was placed inside the church immediately behind the window." On another occasion he recalled, "The first thing I remember after getting inside the fort was seeing Mrs. Melton making circles on the ground with an umbrella. I had seen very few umbrellas." Mrs. Melton, the former Juana Francisca Losoya, had recently married Eliel Melton, the Alamo's quartermaster, the officer in charge of supplies. Her mother and a brother Juan, who was not much older than Enrique, also occupied the Alamo. An older brother, Toribio, served in the garrison and would fight alongside Enrique's father.

Enrique was roaming around the Alamo at dusk when he saw a soldier named Antonio Fuentes speaking to another member of the garrison. The other man asked Fuentes, "Did you know they had cut off the water?" meaning that Mexican soldiers had blocked a ditch bringing fresh water into the fort. The garrison would be forced to surrender if there was no water to drink or to cool the cannons while firing. However, the next morning Enrique saw men drawing water from a well dug a little to the southwest of the center of the Alamo's main plaza. So, the concern about water passed.

On the night that the Esparzas arrived, Enrique's father left the Alamo with a group of men. They took a Mexican soldier prisoner and brought him back with them. During the siege the Texans made this soldier interpret for them the Mexican Army's bugle calls so they would know what moves the enemy intended. Shortly after this, Santa Anna sent a messenger calling for the Alamo's surrender. The Texans answered with a cannon shot.

Enrique would have loved to run around and explore the Alamo, but he could not. Although actual fighting did not happen every day, the two sides exchanged cannon fire, with the Mexican Army dropping a shot into the fort every fifteen minutes.

Both sides settled into the siege as the Mexican soldiers set up artillery positions and slowly encircled the Alamo. President Santa Anna—known as General Santa Anna when in the field—came north with his army personally to direct the war against Texas. He ordered a red flag to be raised over the San Fernando Church in San Antonio to indicate that no mercy would be shown the Texans inside the Alamo.

Enrique saw little of the Alamo's two commanders, Bowie and Travis. Forty-year-old Jim Bowie, known for his frontier adventures and the large knife he carried, became sick on the first day of the siege. He had given over full command to William Travis when the illness confined him to bed. Twenty-seven-year-old Travis now had complete command of the Alamo, without the older Bowie's advice or help. Travis knew that the Alamo could not hold out against the ever-increasing number of Mexican soldiers arriving, so he sent out his own calls for reinforcements and help.

Enrique remembered another American in the Alamo, the famous David Crockett of Tennessee, known to his friends as Davy. "I remember Crockett. He was a tall, slim man, with black whiskers. He was always at the head. . . . He would often come to the fire and warm his hands and say a few words to us in the Spanish language." Later Enrique added, "There was a great cheering when Señor Crockett came with his friends. He wore a buckskin suit and a coonskin cap. He made everybody laugh and forget their troubles. He had a gun called 'Betsey.' They told me that he had killed many bears."

Besides the Esparzas and the Losoyas, other families occupied the Alamo. Enrique recalled Mrs. Juana Navarro Alsbury, her eighteen-month-old son, Alejo, and her sister, Gertrudis Navarro. He mentioned Mrs. Susannah Dickinson, along with her young daughter, Angelina. Susannah's husband, Almeron, served as one of the Alamo's artillery officers. Enrique also remembered a Mrs. Victoriana de Salinas and her three little girls. He remained friends with two of these girls in later years. An older woman called Doña Petra and a younger girl, Trinidad Saucedo, who Enrique thought very pretty, also occupied the Alamo.

A messenger arrived after the first few days, bringing word of reinforcements on their way to the Alamo. The Texans celebrated this news with music from a flute and drums. After a week of skirmishing, there was a three-day truce, during which the Texans considered an offer by Santa Anna. Enrique heard a soldier he described as Badio [Badillo] explain to Enrique's father that Santa Anna had offered the Americans a chance to escape with their lives if they surrendered, but the Mexicans within the Alamo would not be treated so generously. They would be treated as rebels, which meant death. Enrique's father urged his mother to escape with the children, but she refused, saying, "No! If you're going to stay, so am I. If they kill one, they can kill us all."

At least one and possibly two small reinforcements made it into the fort. They lifted the spirits of the men inside, but they did not strengthen the garrison sufficiently. The fighting resumed after the truce ended. Enrique heard music coming from the Mexican camp one night, and the prisoner explained that it meant enemy reinforcements had arrived. Time was growing short for those inside the Alamo.

Young Enrique envied the men who stood with his father and also some boys who were not much older than he. "If I had been given a weapon I would have fought likewise. But weapons and ammunition were scarce and only wielded and used by those who knew how."

The siege dragged on for twelve days, with little rest for the soldiers and families inside. Enrique described the days as "long and full of terror," and the nights as "longer and fraught with still more horror."

"The end came suddenly and almost unexpectedly and with a rush," he stated of the pre-dawn hours of March 6, 1836. His father was not serving on the walls that night but sleeping with his family. Gunfire erupting at the northwest corner of the Alamo compound awakened the Esparzas. "Gregorio, the soldiers have jumped the wall. The fight's begun," Enrique's mother cried. His father jumped up, grabbed his weapons, and went to meet the enemy. Enrique never saw him alive again.

Most of the women and children huddled in the corners of a room within the Alamo church. They heard the cries of soldiers and gunfire raging all around. Mexican troops, charging over the Alamo's walls, fought their way through building after building and room after room. The outnumbered Texans fought valiantly but were unable to hold back the overwhelming numbers against them.

Soon enemy soldiers appeared at the door of the room in which the noncombatants sheltered. They did not know that women and children were there and fired in blindly, thinking that Texan soldiers had taken cover within the room. Enrique remembered a young boy, wrapped in a blanket, who was hit and killed by their bullets. Shortly after sunrise, the gunfire died down and Mexican troops searched the rooms for any surviving Texans. A Mexican soldier entered the Alamo church and pointed a bayonet at Enrique's mother. "Where's the money the Americans had?" he demanded. His mother remained defiant, "If they had any you may look for it," she answered. The soldier struck her and Enrique screamed. An officer appeared and said, "What are you doing? The women and children are not to be hurt." He ordered the women to collect their families and belongings.

Later soldiers escorted the families to the house of Ramón Musquiz on the Main Plaza in San Antonio. There ten to twelve women and children waited together in a room, in fear of what would become of them. But after a while they became very hungry and restless, since they had not eaten. Ana Esparza became their leader. She knew the Musquiz family and their home. She left the room to search for food. Musquiz, fearing for her safety, told her of the danger of moving about. She told him that she did not care. She intended to feed her family and companions, even if Santa Anna did not feed his prisoners. The nervous Musquiz made her return to her room and had coffee, meat, bread, and tamales brought to the women and children.

Later that afternoon, the women and children went before Santa Anna, one family at a time. While the Esparzas waited, young Juan Losoya approached Mrs. Esparza. He delivered a message from his sister, Juana Francisca, asking that Mrs. Esparza not mention to Santa Anna that Juana had married an American. Mrs. Esparza assured Juan that she would not. This surprised Enrique, since Juana Francisca had never before acknowledged his mother as a friend or acquaintance.

When the Esparza family's time had come, they stood before Santa Anna as he questioned Ana. Satisfied that neither they nor any other members of their family were a threat to Mexico, he gave Ana two silver dollars and a blanket, as he would to each of the women, and sent them on their way. They went to the home of one of Enrique's uncles. He remembered his mother weeping for many days and nights afterward.

Enrique's uncle Francisco belonged to the Presidial Company of Béxar, part of the Mexican Army. When Cos's force had left San Antonio the previous December, Enrique's uncle, along with other soldiers who lived in San Antonio, had been allowed to remain there. Santa Anna ordered these men to be ready for service when he arrived, but he did not call on them to take part in the battle. Francisco went to General Cos, who had returned to San Antonio with Santa Anna, and asked permission to find his brother Gregorio's body among the Texan dead. Cos granted his request and Francisco, along with two other brothers, found Gregorio's body in one of the Alamo rooms. He later reported that Gregorio bore a bullet to his breast and a sword wound to his side. They removed his body to El Campo Santo, the burial ground on the west side of San Pedro Creek, where it remains today in an unmarked grave. Enrique, his mother, brothers, and sister did not witness his father's burial. Mexican soldiers burned the rest of the Alamo fighters' bodies.

After his victory at the Alamo, Santa Anna pursued Texan forces as they traveled eastward, under the command of General Sam Houston. Six weeks later, he cornered the Texans at a place called San Jacinto. However, Houston and his men turned the tables, and in a surprise attack lasting only eighteen minutes, defeated the Mexican Army and took Santa Anna prisoner. Texas won her freedom from Mexico and became an independent nation—the Republic of Texas— until 1845, when it joined the United States of America as the twenty-eighth state.

Enrique Esparza grew to adulthood in and around San Antonio, working as a farmer and truck gardener. He married Gertrude Hernandez and raised a family of five girls and two boys. The Alamo grew in fame as one of America's greatest battles, a symbol of bravery and self-sacrifice in the name of freedom. But Enrique never shared his thoughts and memories of the battle until the early 1900s, when the new century brought renewed interest in the country's past.

Newspaper reporters sought out Enrique, now an elderly man, and printed several interviews with him over the years. He also visited a classroom and spoke to students about the Alamo. Their teacher later published his story in a book, one hundred years after the battle.

Enrique passed away on December 20, 1917, in Losoya, Texas, at the age of eighty-nine and is buried in El Carmen Cemetery in Losoya, approximately 13.5 miles from the Alamo.

The accounts left by Enrique vary to a degree or have contradictory information. We do not know if he became forgetful or confused in his old age, or if those recording his story misunderstood him and added details of their own. He, however, remained confident in his memories of the Alamo. As he stated to an interviewer in 1907, "You ask me do I remember it. I tell you yes. It is burned into my brain and indelibly seared there. Neither age nor infirmity could make me forget...."

Katie Jennings and John Jenkins:
Young Heroes for Texas Independence

Easy Jackson

General Sam Houston, Davy Crockett, Jim Bowie—theirs are the famous stories in the fight for Texas independence. They were all grown men when they fought for freedom from Mexico, yet some young Texans, too, were just as patriotic and willing to help as their elders. Catherine "Katie" Jennings was ten years old and John Holland Jenkins was thirteen when the fighting began and their courage was tested. They probably knew, too, that their homeland was no stranger to battle.

Centuries before Katie and John were born, American Indian tribes had roamed in and out of the land we now call "Texas." And from 1519 to 1848, the land was claimed by many different countries—France, Spain, Mexico, and the United States. Beginning in the early 1800s, Spain controlled Mexico, which then included all of Texas. Then in 1821, Mexico won its independence from Spain. At first, settlers living in Texas rejoiced, hoping to have a better government than the earlier Spanish one. And in the beginning, all went well. But in the next fifteen years, the Mexican government changed dramatically. Its 1824 constitution was overthrown and replaced with a dictatorship under General Santa Anna. A selfish man, he was so ambitious that he claimed, "If I were God, I would wish to be more."

Santa Anna, governing from Mexico City, demanded that Texans give up their arms. He also denied them the right to trial by jury and failed to provide a system of public schools. In protest, 189 Texans occupied the Alamo mission in the town of San Antonio.

On February 23, 1836, General Santa Anna arrived in San Antonio and surrounded the Alamo with a mighty army of 1,800 Mexican troops. The general wanted not only to conquer the Texan rebels but to crush them. He hoisted a blood-red banner on top of the bell tower of a nearby church. With sinking hearts, the Texans knew what it meant—*deguello*, or "no quarter." Santa Anna would show no mercy. "In this war, you know," he wrote, "there are no prisoners."

General Sam Houston and his forces made camp at the base of this live oak during their retreat from Gonzales, often called the "Runaway Scrape." LIBRARY OF CONGRESS PRINTS AND PHOTOGRAPHS DIVISION, HIGHSMITH (CAROL M.) ARCHIVE

In defiance, the men inside the Alamo fired a cannon. Santa Anna's soldiers answered by bombarding the mission with artillery and cannon fire. Colonel William B. Travis, commander of the Texans inside the Alamo, vowed "victory or death," and David Crockett, Jim Bowie, and many others agreed. One of those who refused to give up was Gordon C. Jennings, a man in his fifties, whose wife and four children lived near Bastrop, Texas. For twelve days, Santa Anna's army besieged the Alamo. On the thirteenth day, Mexican forces overran its walls. All the Texan men inside were killed in bloody hand-to-hand combat, including Gordon Jennings. But the men's bravery had bought General Sam Houston, commander in chief of all the Texan forces, thirteen days to help form a new republic—the Republic of Texas—and to gather enough soldiers to fight Santa Anna's army.

News of the fall of the Alamo—and of Santa Anna's intentions of slaughtering Texans—began to spread among the settlers. All who remained on the home front now were the older, weaker men, along with the women and children. Rumors flew. Then came the news that Santa Anna's army had killed everyone in the town of Goliad. The settlers panicked. Frightened women, children, and old men realized that their only hope was to bolt to the Texas-Louisiana border to escape the coming army. This mass flight, in the cold rain and mud and across rising creeks and rivers, became known as "the Runaway Scrape."

When Gordon Jennings's wife learned of the fall of the Alamo, she mourned for her dead husband. But she realized that to protect herself and her children, she would have to act right away. She sent her older children to free the livestock and started to pack the family's belongings, all the while worrying aloud that some of the neighbors might not have heard the terrible news.

Without hesitating, ten-year-old Katie Jennings offered to ride to the surrounding neighbors and warn them of Santa Anna's approach. Despite the bitter weather, her mother quickly bridled the family's best horse and lifted Katie onto its back. She instructed her daughter to head out with the last people she visited. The Jennings family members would catch up with one another on route to Louisiana. "No matter what," Mrs. Jennings ordered Katie, "don't come back here."

Riding like the wind on a bareback horse, her pigtails flying behind her, Katie raced to give warning. From cabin to cabin through slippery mud she rode, never knowing if she was riding straight into an advancing Mexican Army, or if she'd find a band of Indians around the next bend. Settler after settler heard Katie's news and began to flee from the destruction sure to come their way. Some of them even left food on the table, not daring to take the time to do anything but run.

There is no way to know how many lives Katie saved. And it would be weeks before she met up with her family again. But "The Ride of Katie Jennings" became a Texas legend.

The famous ride would not be Katie's only act of bravery. While still a teenager, she married a man named Caspar Whistler and moved to present-day Collin County, Texas. There the couple shared a cabin with Wesley Clemmons and his wife. Early in the afternoon of Christmas Day 1842, Caspar and Wesley left the cabin to finish some work nearby. Soon they were jumped by screaming Indians. Katie grabbed a gun but failed to get it to Caspar. She and Mrs. Clemmons watched in horror as their husbands, unable to defend themselves, were shot, tomahawked, scalped, and mutilated.

Although the Indians fled after the killings, the sobbing women dared not leave their cabin until evening. Mrs. Clemmons decided to stay in the cabin, guarding her two children and the bodies of the men outside. Katie waited for nightfall and crept out of the cabin to get help. The nearest neighbor had built a fort eight miles away, but there was no road. Katie's only choice was to follow a dry creek bed. Unable to see clearly—and terrified of being discovered by the Indians—Katie plodded on, determined to save herself, her friend, and her friend's children. Briars and thorns tore her clothes and made such deep scratches in her skin that she would bear the scars the rest of her life. After stumbling and falling many times, almost naked and crying in grief and pain, Katie finally found the fort. At daybreak, men from the settlement returned to the cabin and rescued Mrs. Clemmons and her children. They also took up the bodies of the murdered men for burial.

One of the rescuers, a young man named Sylvester Lockwood, fell in love with Katie. The two married in 1843, while Texas was still a struggling young republic. Although Sylvester was unable to write his name, with Katie's help, he became a successful businessman. Kindhearted and generous, the two took in many orphans during the course of their lives. "There is always room for one more," they believed.

Although her life was filled with adventure, Katie loved most to tell the stories of the spring of 1836 and the days of the Texas Revolution. "She would tell of her father's death at the Alamo, of her family's struggle to survive during the Runaway Scrape, and of her heart-pounding ride," wrote Lee Spence, Katie's great-great-great-great granddaughter. On the day of Katie's ride, said this relative, "another hero of the Texas Revolution emerged."

John Holland Jenkins was a thirteen-year-old Bastrop boy when Katie Jennings's father died. John's own father had been murdered and scalped four years earlier, but his stepfather was one of the Texans holed up at the Alamo. While the siege was raging, General Edward Burleson was busy gathering forces to fight the Mexican Army. Under Burleson's command, Captain Jesse Billingsley led the "Mina Volunteers" in Company C, which was Burleson's First Regiment of Texas Volunteers for Sam Houston's army. Young John Jenkins was a ward of General Burleson. The boy greatly admired the general's fearlessness, his modesty, and his ability to outwit his enemies. John was remarkably large and stout for his age, and he yearned to be off fighting with Burleson, his hero. So, when Captain Billingsley camped near his home, John persuaded his mother to let him enter the army with the Bastrop men. "As I found myself among old friends and acquaintances, with all of a growing boy's appetite for good beef, bread, and adventure, I thought there had never been such fun as serving as a Texas soldier marching against Mexico," he later wrote.

But much to the disgust of the Texans, Sam Houston kept them marching eastward, away from San Antonio and the Alamo. Many believed that Houston hoped that his old friend President Andrew Jackson would let US army troops slip unofficially over the Louisiana border to help the Texans fight.

While they were camped at Gonzales, Texas, the men learned of the fall of the Alamo. John Jenkins knew that his stepfather had perished with the others. The shrieks of despair from the wives of some of the men who had died affected John greatly. "I now could understand that there is woe in warfare, as well as glory and labor."

Still the Mexican Army kept up its fierce advance. General Burleson now ordered John to return to Bastrop to help his mother and siblings, along with other Texans, to flee the burning and devastation that would surely come. John, along with three other men, rushed to Bastrop, fearing what they would find. "Exposed to the most disagreeable weather, wading by day through mud and water over the very worst of roads, and tentless at night, it was tedious and hard beyond description."

John found his family and the other Bastrop settlers safe. But with the Mexican soldiers pressing near, all were frantic to escape. The roads were terrible. Streams overflowed their banks, and women carrying babies had to cross water that was waist deep. But John and the other men General Burleson had sent stayed with the settlers and offered them help and protection.

John was not able to be with Captain Billingsley when the captain led the Bastrop men into battle against the Mexican Army at San Jacinto. Neither did John hear Billingsley scream, "Remember the Alamo! Remember Goliad!" Still the Texans considered John an important part of that fearful campaign. They believed the boy to be "in the most honorable sense a San Jacinto soldier." He was also the youngest one to serve.

When news of the Texans' victory reached John and his family, they returned to Bastrop. They found it deserted and sacked—robbed—of everything except a few hogs. John began to help his mother rebuild the family's life, and when she died, he took responsibility for his siblings. But life on the frontier continued to be violent.

At one point, Comanche Indians were stealing horses from settlers in Bastrop on a weekly basis, and John earned a reputation as an exceptional Indian fighter. The Tonkawa Indians hated other tribes and often sided with the whites against them. After John had been forced to kill a Waco Indian in self-defense, a band of Tonkawas insisted he take them to the body. As John watched in shock, the Tonkawas cut off the dead man's legs and hands, which they later cooked and fed to the Tonkawa women in a ceremony meant to bring success in war.

Despite all he had seen of the brutality of life on the frontier, John Jenkins condemned white men who resorted to extreme cruelty to the Indians. As an old man, he remembered that "Men almost forgot the meaning of love and mercy and forbearance amid the scenes through which we passed in those early days."

Like Katie Jennings, John continued to live a life of courage and honor long after the revolution had ended and Texas had gained statehood. Even so, his end would not be peaceful. In 1890, he died from wounds received in a gunfight in Bastrop as he tried to save his son, Bastrop's sheriff, from an ambush.

Lotta Crabtree: Child Star of the Gold Rush

Chris Enss

A little redheaded girl, dressed as a leprechaun, marched past a group of muddy miners into the center of their rustic camp. Her mother helped her onto a stump while a banjo player strummed a tune for the child, who soon began dancing an Irish jig. The delighted Forty-Niners clapped and cheered for the girl, and she laughed at their enthusiasm. After she finished entertaining the men, they tossed gold nuggets and coins at her feet. She beamed with pride at the applause while her mother collected her earnings and tucked them inside a leather grip. One of the youngest entertainers to travel through the Sierra Mountains in the mid-1800s, Lotta Crabtree's diverse talents and infectious laugh made her a star in the Gold Country, as well as the primary bread-winner for her family.

Lotta was born in New York in 1847 and given the name Charlotte Mignon Crabtree. Her parents, John and Mary Ann Crabtree, ran a bookstore. John, a tall man who sported beaver hats, ignored the business and spent much of his time trying to find a shortcut to getting rich or enjoying "the good life," as he called it, in a saloon. Mary Ann kept the shop afloat, occasionally bringing in money by working as an upholsterer. Her serious, responsible nature was reflected in her manner of dress. She always wore a one-piece, black taffeta, princess-style frock. She knew almost immediately that she had made a mistake when she married John, but she was determined to see it through. Her husband was less dedicated to making the marriage work.

John succumbed to gold fever in 1851 and decided to move west to find his fortune. Little did he know that his daughter would soon be bringing in more gold than he could ever uncover. Mary Ann followed her husband to California in 1852. John was supposed to meet his family in San Francisco, but, true to his character, he never showed up.

Mary Ann found herself alone in a booming metropolis, with no prospects and a child to care for. To think about what to do, she sat down on the docks next to the ship that had brought her there. Her situation wasn't unique. Many wives and children were left stranded in the Gold Country by their husbands and fathers. A man's desire to strike it rich often overruled his obligation

Lotta Crabtree, 1868 LIBRARY OF CONGRESS PRINTS AND PHOTOGRAPHS
DIVISION, J. GURNEY & SON, PHOTOGRAPHER, C. 1868

to his family. Mary Ann stared into the happy, smiling face of her daughter and realized she had to make the best of the circumstances. She appealed for help to a few people whom she had befriended on the ship. She moved in with some of these generous new friends and tried to build a life for herself and her daughter.

Theatrical shows were very popular in San Francisco. The city's various playhouses were always filled with bored miners looking to be amused. As the need for entertainment grew, more performers came to town daily. Variety shows sprang up overnight and featured acrobats, singers, and slapstick comedians. Child actors were held in particularly high regard because they reminded the miners of the sons and daughters they had left behind to search for gold.

Mary Ann loved the theater and took Lotta to see the shows as often as she could. Early in her life, Mary Ann had wanted to be a performer, but she had abandoned that dream to get married. She watched the actors, singers, and dancers with great admiration and kept a close eye on how many people were in the audience. She noticed that the Forty-Niners were willing to pay handsomely to see the shows, and she wanted to get in on the act. It wasn't long before she became friends with a circle of the most popular actors of the nineteenth century. Her plan was to use them to transform her vibrant, talented, bubbly little girl into a star. Mary Ann enrolled Lotta in a dance class and encouraged her daughter's acting aspirations.

John Crabtree finally contacted his wife in 1853 and begged for her forgiveness. He confessed that he had found nothing but a few flakes of gold while panning in the creek beds around Sutter's Mill. He pleaded with Mary Ann to join him in Grass Valley, California, where he had it in his mind to run a boardinghouse for miners. Mary Ann reluctantly agreed to follow her husband. She was less than impressed with the gold-mining town when she arrived.

Grass Valley was no San Francisco. It had a population of only 3,500. Three hundred were women, and fifteen were school-age children. The town was rustic and lacked many of the opportunities she wanted Lotta to have. She helped John open their second-class, two-story boardinghouse on Main Street and enrolled Lotta in the only dancing school around. The classes were conducted in the annex of a tavern.

Jared Reynolds was Lotta's dance instructor, and he was quite taken with her abilities. Many of the miners who stopped in the saloon for a drink gathered around to watch her twirl across the tiny stage. Tears would well up in their eyes as they thought of their own children, and they would shower the tot with chunks of gold and other gifts of appreciation.

Half of California's foreign-born population was Irish in the 1850s. Jared knew this and made sure his pupil could dance jigs and reels—dances very popular in Ireland. One day, soon after she had mastered those dances, the dance instructor loaded Lotta in a buggy, and without asking her parents, took off for the gold fields. When she didn't return home after class that evening, Mary Ann and John were frantic. Their first child, Harriet, had died in infancy, and this naturally made them protective of Lotta.

After a few hours, Jared returned the child to her home with news that her dancing had been a huge hit with the miners in the hills. He wanted to organize a musical troupe and escort Lotta around the gold fields with the other entertainers. Mary Ann wasn't in the mood to hear his plan. She was furious with Jared for taking Lotta without permission and reprimanded him for his actions. John thought Jared's idea had promise.

Jared Reynolds wasn't the only one who took a special interest in Lotta. Lola Montez, the notorious entertainer who had gained international fame performing the Spider Dance, thought the child had great potential. Lola lived a few doors away from the Crabtree's boardinghouse, and she spent many hours teaching Lotta some of her dance steps and how to ride a horse. Lola adored Lotta and let her play with her costumes and dance to her German music box. She pleaded with Mary Ann to let her take the energetic child to Australia with her, to tour the country. Mary Ann, who was expecting another child at the time, refused. She was, however, encouraged by Lola's interest in Lotta. She enrolled Lotta in more dance classes and added singing classes to her studies. By the age of ten, Lotta was one of the most talented children in the Gold Country. She had a wonderful voice, a great sense of comic timing, and was a master of dances like the fandango and the Highland Fling.

Just when it seemed that Lotta's craft was being perfected, John moved his family from Grass Valley and headed north to a town called Rabbit Creek. After opening up another boardinghouse, he left his wife and two children for another gold search. Mary Ann was left to handle the business again. She resented cleaning up after unwashed, dirty miners. She knew that Lotta was the answer to a better life.

During her stay in Rabbit Creek, Mary Ann met Mart Taylor, a musician and dancer who managed a saloon and crude theater where traveling players often appeared. Mary Ann convinced him to let Lotta perform for his customers. Lotta danced and sang a couple of sentimental ballads. She was a hit, and Mart quickly took her under his supervision. An actor in the audience, Walter Leman, saw Lotta's performance and was impressed with her skill. He made a note of it in his journal. "How thou didst squirm and do a walk around and do all with impunity and vim that defied all opposition and criticism," Walter recalled. "For thou were bright and merry, and everybody loved to see thee, laugh at the capers, enjoy thy fun, and toss into thee lap the coins and nuggets of the land of gold."

Mart and Mary Ann quickly put together a company of musicians and set off to travel the various mining camps with their pint-sized gold mine. Lotta was well received wherever the troupe went, and she earned more than thirteen dollars a night dancing and singing.

Highwaymen would lie in wait to steal from entertainers. One night, the infamous bandit of the Sierras, Black Bart, stopped the group and demanded their money. Lotta's banjo player, Jake Wallace, was petrified and scrawled in his diary what happened after the robber ordered them off their horses. Wallace wrote, "He walked out of the trees over to us. He was a big man dressed in a long coat with a watch chain coming out of the pocket. We waren't [sic] what he expected. When he found out we waren't [sic] the mail, he let us go. We parted as good friends."

Lotta's father, again, was unable to strike it rich. He joined the troupe and toured with them for a time. He was amazed at the reaction his daughter received in the mining camps. She was greeted by thunderous applause, followed by showers of coins and nuggets. He'd not seen that much gold in all the time he had been prospecting. Mary Ann knew that Lotta's act could earn more money in big city theaters. This time it was Mary Ann who decided to move the family back to San Francisco.

Lotta performed at variety halls and amusement parks and soon became known as the "San Francisco Favorite." She was twelve and the sole supporter of her family, which now included two brothers.

Mary Ann was in charge of every aspect of Lotta's career. She made her costumes, applied her makeup, booked her into the various performance halls, and made sure the schedule allowed for Lotta to take parts in plays at the better theaters in San Francisco. She handled all of Lotta's money as well, insisting on getting Lotta's share after the box office closed each night, rather than wait until the end of the week. She had a mortal fear of theater fires. A theater's gas footlights could, and often did, explode and cause a fire that, in a matter of minutes, would consume a building and its contents.

Lotta was devoted to her mother. Her high spirits and irrepressible good humor on stage reflected Mary Ann's boundless confidence in her. Mary Ann prevented Lotta from having any intimate contacts or lasting friends, though. She believed that any outside influence would jeopardize the golden treasure she had helped create. Lotta was totally dependent on her mother, and that was just the way Mary Ann wanted it.

Under the watchful eye of her mother, Lotta was hustled directly to performances and home again, and, although she was approaching sixteen, there were still no boyfriends. Mary Ann made a habit of intervening and heading off any romance that might come Lotta's way. A supporting player in one of the stage plays in which Lotta performed said that she was "guarded like an odalisque in a harem." Most people referred to the cheerful Lotta as "Miss Lotta, the Unapproachable." Once, toward evening in the summer, a young man with a horse and carriage called to take her riding. Mary Ann sent him away quickly, but, for days afterward following dinner, Lotta contrived to sweep the front porch in case he should return. Much to Lotta's chagrin, he did not.

Lotta Crabtree was a popular star and in constant demand. By 1863, she was earning more than forty-two thousand dollars a year. Mary Ann was a smart businesswoman and invested her daughter's money in real estate. She walked the streets of the towns Lotta performed in and bought vacant lots that she believed would be highly sought after as the town grew. Lotta had no head for finances and counted on her mother to pay all her bills and support her act.

At the height of Lotta's fame in California, Lotta, Mary Ann, and her brothers, George and Ashworth, traveled east. Lotta captured the hearts of theatergoers in New York, Chicago, Boston, and the Midwest. She performed in *Uncle Tom's Cabin* and *Jenny Leatherlungs*. One of her most popular plays was an adaptation of Dickens's *The Old Curiosity Shop*, in which Lotta played two different characters. In *The Little Detective*, she impersonated six characters. Lotta was fond of portraying young men. She had such a youthful face that she could get away with playing those kinds of roles, but her mother objected. Mary Ann thought her child should be portraying queens and damsels in distress, but Lotta had an unladylike habit of plunging her hands into the pants of her costumes. To combat this, Mary Ann sewed the pockets shut on her entire wardrobe.

Her mother's overbearing actions never dampened Lotta's spirit. Lotta was thrilled with the praise she received from the audiences on the East Coast. In a letter to a friend in 1865, she wrote how she felt about the reception she was getting everywhere she performed: "I'm a continual success wherever I go. In some places I created quite a theatrical furor as they call it. I performed in Buffalo in a play called 'Fanchon.' The people were delighted, and the theater not big enough to hold them. . . . Why, friend Billie, your heart would jump for joy to see the respect I am treated with here among the theater people. I'm a star and that is sufficient, and making quite a name."

Even in her thirties Lotta would always give the impression of being a young girl, never a woman, but a girl who delighted in flouting convention. She wore her skirts shorter than most, smoked thinly rolled black cigars, and sprinkled her hair with cayenne pepper in order to catch the reflection of the footlights.

By 1870, Lotta was earning eighty thousand dollars a year and was one of the most popular actresses on the American stage. She spent a great deal of the allowance her mother gave her on her family, lavishing them with gold watches and fine clothes and sending her brothers to the best schools in the country. Mary Ann kept track of every dime Lotta spent and was convinced that if she didn't keep a close eye on her, the very generous Lotta would give away all the money she had.

On one occasion Lotta borrowed a dollar from her business manager, Eddie Dunn. She misplaced the money and then, feeling guilty about it, confessed to her mother what she had done. Mary Ann cornered Dunn and gave him a tongue-lashing. "Mr. Dunn, Miss Lotta told me you gave her a dollar the other day, a dollar which she promptly lost. Never again give her more than ten cents at one time. She has no knowledge of money, nor has need for it."

Mary Ann was the quintessential stage mother. She was so protective of Lotta and her fortune that she would fight anyone to keep both intact. She once caught her husband stealing coins from the steamer trunk where she stored Lotta's earnings. She was so outraged by his behavior that she had him arrested. Mary Ann felt John's actions would have a negative effect on Lotta's career and agreed not to press charges if he would leave the country. John reluctantly left for England.

Lotta and her mother toured Europe in 1874 and returned to America and the theater in 1875. At twenty-eight, Lotta was still portraying children and playing young parts in comical performances. She loved making people laugh. Lotta loved animals, too, and when she finally returned to her beloved San Francisco to perform in yet another play, she purchased a fountain at the intersection of Kearney and Market Streets and donated it to the city so that thirsty horses would have a place to get a drink.

Lotta retired from the theater at the age of forty-five. She was tired and wanted a chance to rest and enjoy the money she had made. She and her mother retreated to a summer cottage on Lake Hopatcong, New Jersey. She named the cottage Attol Tryst. ("Attol" is "Lotta" spelled backward.) Although it was a gift from mother to daughter, it was built with Lotta's money. It was one of the most elaborate homes in the area.

Mary Ann Crabtree died in 1905. Lotta was grief-stricken. Her constant companion and best friend was no longer at her side. Mary Ann didn't leave a will, but Lotta found more than seventy thousand dollars in cash hidden throughout their home. Twenty thousand of that was hidden inside a granite coffeepot. Lotta also found financial statements that showed the amount of money she had earned from the investments her mother had made for her. Mary Ann's investments had brought in more than two million dollars.

Lotta sold the mansion on Lake Hopatcong and purchased a home in Boston, where she lived a quiet, almost reclusive life. The remaining years of her life were spent painting and giving her money away. On many days, she could be found on the streets of Boston, fitting straw hats on horses to shade them from the heat.

Lotta Crabtree died of arteriosclerosis, or hardening of the arteries, in 1924 at the age of seventy-seven, and was buried next to her mother in Woodlawn Cemetery in New York City. She left her estate, estimated at four million dollars, to veterans, animals, students of music and agriculture, needy children at Christmas, and needy actors. Most historians consider her one of the theater's first comediennes.

Boys on the Trail:
Surviving on Bark and Burnt Rawhide

Candy Moulton

Heber leaned toward the small campfire, shivering as snow stuck to the shoulders of his thin coat. He took the piece of cattlehide he had been holding over the flames. It was now crispy, so he let it cool and then drew a string of it through his teeth to get some of the burnt scales off. He and other boys his age and younger were desperately hungry. They were all drawing the rawhide through the fire, then chewing on it for any bit of nourishment they could get.

Sometimes Heber just sat and stared at the flames. The flickering light mesmerized him and took him back to a time when he was not cold. Back to when he was excited to be on a great adventure . . .

Preparations for his family's grand journey to America were in full swing when Heber McBride turned thirteen on May 13, 1856. In just over a week, the McBrides would be in Liverpool, England, loading their possessions onto the *Horizon*, a three-mast clipper ship that would carry them and 850 other emigrants to New York City.

The *Horizon* left the Bramley-Moore Dock, Port of Liverpool, and slowly sailed into the River Mersey. The ship's crew soon cast anchor to allow government officers and doctors to climb on board and check the people and their goods. After the inspection, the crew began quarreling, and their fight became so rough that the first officer pulled out a gun and threatened to shoot. A signal brought policemen to the ship. They put iron handcuffs on the fighting crew members and escorted them to shore.

Heber and his little brothers, Ether, who was eight, and Peter, who was six, watched with wide-eyed wonder. Heber had expected excitement as part of the family journey from England to America and their ultimate destination in Great Salt Lake City, where the church they belonged to had its headquarters. But he did not anticipate a fight among the crew before the men even ran the sails up the three masts on the ship that would take the family across the Atlantic Ocean.

An engraving of Chimney Rock, Nebraska LIBRARY OF CONGRESS PRINTS AND PHOTOGRAPHS DIVISION, FREDERICK HAWKINS PIERCY, 1830–1891, ARTIST

When the clipper glided away from England and onto the open ocean, it rocked and rolled. Many of the travelers were ill from the motion. Heber loved the great waves. "I was in my element all the time and the harder the wind did blow the better I enjoyed myself." He and the other boys on the ship watched sperm whales breeching and flipping their V-notched tails, called flukes, into the air.

One day a school of dolphins trailed beside the ship, their backs showing above the surface of the sea-green water. "They resembled a band of horses on the run. This attitude gave me the name of the seahorse. It was a wonderful sight. It seemed to fill a space of half a mile square," traveler John Southwell recalled. Another time, the lookout saw a huge whale and people rushed to the deck. At that moment, the skies were filled with a thousand rainbows, as the whale blew and spouted water, causing the spray to glisten in the sun.

Even more thrilling, days later, those on the ship saw "a large man-eating shark." The monster quickly turned and disappeared, but a huge wave brought it to the surface. Anticipating this action, the mate fired his rifle, striking the shark. An old sailor instantly launched his harpoon. The metal flashed as it struck the shark, which made a few terrific lunges. But the harpoon, attached to the ship with a strong rope, held. The creature was subdued after a furious struggle. The sailors now used a block and tackle to hoist the shark aboard. When it came to rest on the deck, the men laid a line along his carcass, determining that the shark was thirty feet long. The old whaler thought he weighed about 2,500 pounds. The shark was bigger than anything Heber McBride had ever seen before. It had a gaping mouth, showing rows of sharp teeth. The sightings of sharks, porpoises, and whales were astounding wonders to the lad.

The *Horizon* docked in New York Harbor, and Heber's family members gathered their goods and left the ship. They were now roughly a third of the way to their destination. They boarded a train for a two-week trip to Iowa City, Iowa. There the real trail experiences would start.

For several months, Mormon men in America had been planning for the hundreds of travelers who were with the group Heber and his family had joined. Edward Martin led the travelers' company. They called him Captain. In Iowa, the Mormons built the two-wheeled carts that Heber's family and others would fill with their clothing, cooking utensils, bedding, and the food that they would need for the next stage of their journey. Now they were expected to pull and push the small handcarts for well over 1,200 miles on the trail that earlier members of the Mormon Church had followed into the West to the Great Salt Lake Valley.

Prior to 1856, Mormon families had used wagons pulled by teams of oxen to transport their goods and themselves from areas near the Mississippi and Missouri Rivers. But now there was not enough money to buy enough wagons and teams for everyone wanting to travel west. Brigham Young, the president of the church, told the people they should use small, two-wheeled handcarts and walk to their destination in Great Salt Lake City.

In addition to his brothers, Heber traveled with his father, Robert; mother, Margaret Ann; sixteen-year-old sister, Janetta; and baby sister, Margaret Alice, who was just two years old. They loaded their handcart, a small vehicle about three feet square, with a box just over a foot deep. It had bent pieces of wood, called bows, that formed a top, which was covered with a white canvas. The carts looked like miniature prairie wagons, except that instead of a tongue that could be attached to a team of oxen or mules, they had a front bar that people could get behind to push, or walk in front of and pull. With their personal items and Margaret Alice tucked into the cart, Heber's family walked away from Iowa City in late July. The first few weeks on the trail they spent in Iowa, going up and then down the many hills on the rough path that served as the road west. They crossed the Missouri River in mid-August and rested for a few days in eastern Nebraska.

It was very late in the summer, and they hesitated to start out for Great Salt Lake City since they knew it would take at least two months to walk there with the carts. They heard some people argue that they should stay in eastern Nebraska, but others insisted that they could complete their journey before it got too cold and snowy winter weather set in. Heber and his family, like most of their fellow travelers, had no idea what to expect, but they did know that their new homes were farther west.

They listened to but did not heed the warnings. Instead, in late August, the McBride family picked up their cart and continued walking, traveling ten to fifteen miles every day, always facing toward where the sun set in the evening. They had food they believed would be enough to last for two months. The weather was still very hot. Hands, faces, and lips became sunburned, chapped, and sore. Their shoes began to wear out, and every step was harder than the one before it.

"Mother took chills and fever then our trouble began," Heber recalled. "She would walk as far as she could by holding on to the cart then we would get her in to one of the wagons." There were only a few wagons with the handcart company. Pulled by oxen, the wagons carried some supplies, and sometimes weary or ill people could get a ride. The carts became rickety. They had been built using newly cut, green lumber. As the wood dried out, the wheels on the carts began to squeal and then to fall apart. Captain Martin's company had to stop frequently to make repairs. Sometimes they took their bacon, and instead of cooking and eating it, they rubbed it on the axles of the carts to make them roll easier—and to quit screeching. Sooner than they expected, their food grew scarce. Then the soil turned to sand, and the carts' wheels sank into it. Walking was harder and harder each day. Heber said, "the men began to give out, teams gave out, and so many [people] sick and dieing that they couldent all ride."

As if it wasn't bad enough that Heber's mother was ill, soon his father began struggling from the travel. More of the responsibility for the family now fell to Heber and his sister Janetta. The children pushed and pulled the handcart through the soft ground, struggling more each day. Heber and Janetta warned their younger brothers to watch out for prickly pear. The cactus grew well in the sandy soil and dry climate of western Nebraska. It covered the ground, just waiting to stab anyone who misplaced a foot. Western Nebraska also offered curious natural features and sandstone outcrops such as Chimney Rock, Ancient Bluff, Courthouse, and Jail Rocks. But all the walking took a toll.

"Sometimes we would find Mother laying by the side of the road," Heber recalled. "We would get her on the cart and haul her along till we would find Father lying as if he was dead then Mother would be rested a little and she would try and walk and Father would get on and ride and then we used to cry and feel so bad." Many days the McBride family did not reach camp until after dark, when they would need to "hunt something to make a fire," usually the buffalo chips (manure) they found on the prairie. No one helped the children and their weary, ailing parents. Other families traveling with Captain Martin had their own similar struggles.

Heber feared for his mother's life one rainy night when they reached camp late. "We thought she was going to die and we had gathered a few sunflower stalks and wet Buffloo chips and had just got a little fire started when all hands were ordered to attend prayers and because we did not go to prayers Daniel Tyler came and kicked our fire all out and spilled the water that we was trying to get warm to make a little tea for Mother."

Day after day, the handcart company walked. The weather became colder and colder, while the days became shorter and shorter. Wolves began following the handcart train, howling throughout the night.

Heber's family reached the last crossing of the North Platte River on October 19 and waded through the river's waist-deep water and the mushy chunks of ice floating in it. They were barely across the river when a strong winter storm swirled in from the northwest. As traveler John Jaques later remembered, "Winter came on all at once, and that was the first day of it."

By then Robert McBride was so weak that he could barely sit up. As soon as they had crossed the river, Heber found a place for his father to ride in one of the wagons. Heavy snow was falling when they reached their camp. The wind was blowing and it was bitterly cold. Heber and Janetta pitched their tent and found a few willow branches to burn for heat. After making their mother and the younger children as comfortable as possible, Heber and Janetta went to get their father. "The wind was blowing the snow so bad that we could not see anything and the wagons had not got into camp and it was then after dark so we did not find him that night," Heber said. "The next morning there was about 6 inches of snow on the ground and then what we had to suffer can never be told."

Janetta prepared breakfast while Heber went looking for their father. "Oh Father, Father," the boy cried when he located Robert. The man was "under a wagon with snow all over him and he was stiff and dead. I felt as though my heart would burst." The pain of loss was nearly unbearable. "There we was away out on the Plains with hardly anything to eat and Father dead and mother sick." Heber wailed and cried. But then he dried his eyes and went to the tent to tell his mother, Janetta, and his younger brothers and sister that their father was dead. The boy was now responsible for his family in a way he had never imagined.

Other families also faced unbearable loss. Fathers and mothers were too ill to do much work. Many of them died. The snow and cold weather made it impossible for the people to move their handcarts. The weary travelers could barely keep fires burning. "It seemed as though death would be a blessing," Heber wrote. "Our clothing almost worn out and not enough of bedclothes to keep us warm. We would lay and suffer from night till morning with the cold."

After two months of nonstop walking, they were still hundreds of miles from Great Salt Lake City, and they had eaten almost all of their food. Heber said that his two little brothers "would get the sack that had flour in and turn it wrong side out and suck and lick the flour dust from it." The boys in the handcart caravan found willow bushes, cut off their branches, and stripped the bark so that they could chew on them as a bitter food source.

The company had some oxen, and when an animal died the people would quickly devour the meat. "Us little boys would get strips of rawhide and try and eat it," Heber said. Like the others, he would take a strip of the animal skin and "crisp it in the fire and then draw a string of it through our teeth and get some of the burnt scales off that way and then crisp it again and repeat the operation till we would get tired." It did not taste good, and it did not fill their bellies, but it was all that they had.

Mentally and physically worn down, Martin's group could do little more than huddle together for warmth and pray for aid.

❦

One morning, more than a week after they had crossed the North Platte River, a "big blue winged angel came flying to our rescue," one of the boys said. A woman named Mary Scott saw the rescuers first, jumping to her feet and screaming at the top of her voice, "I see them coming! I see them coming! Surely they are angels from heaven." As the people in camp came out of their tents and looked westward, they saw three men on horses. The rescuers had a pack mule with a few supplies that they shared among the company. More important, they gave the people hope, telling them that some sixty miles farther west, at a place called Devil's Gate, they would find wagons filled with food, warm bedding, and clothing.

The cold and snow continued, and food was still extremely scarce, but Heber's family and fellow travelers picked up their carts and continued the journey. They struggled up hills and across the windswept landscape. They passed Independence Rock and finally reached Devil's Gate and the rescue supplies. It was now late October, and there was not enough food for them to stay at Devil's Gate for the winter. After several days, though, the weather improved. Now the families knew they had to get back on the trail.

Because the rescue party had wagons and teams, many of the people abandoned their carts and found a place to ride when they left Devil's Gate. Heber, Janetta, and Ether helped their mother and younger brother and sister into a wagon, but the youngsters walked the rest of the way to Great Salt Lake City. They arrived on November 30. The grand adventure had taken six months, caused unbearable loss, and Heber was glad it was over. Now he and his family would build a new life in America.

Pony Trail Tales

Quackgrass Sally

Billy slowly ran his hand down the neck of the horse, the warm velvet feel calming his heart as much as his touch soothed the horse. It was April 3, 1860, almost 5:00 p.m. The sound of the growing crowd outside the tall wooden stable doors reminded Billy that today he had to do his best. His saddle felt snug and the cinch was tight. He needed to remember when he mounted to throw his leg wide to clear those locked mochila pockets filled with mail. No mistakes. There would be a lot of people watching. Why, even the newspaper reporters were supposed to be gathering here from all over the territory. Rumor hinted that they are headlining this "an historic event." Billy didn't want to think about that. All he knew was that he had to ride swift and sure. Sit tight in the saddle and keep the horse moving. Soon they would swing open those stable doors and he'd be headed west, riding for the Central Overland PONY EXPRESS!

Pushing out of his eyes a wisp of hair that had escaped from under his hat brim, Billy still couldn't believe *he'd* be the first rider out of St. Joseph, Missouri. Why, even Della Richardson, who had been at the stables the night the four XP, or Pony Express, riders drew straws, would be mighty surprised when she saw Billy in the saddle.

"Those boys drew straws to determine who was to be the first pony rider," she later told the newspapers. "Johnny Frye drew the shortest straw, so he was going to be the first. But, lo and behold, Johnny injured himself yesterday when he was attempting to ride an untrained horse. He was thrown and badly sprained his wrist. Since Billy had drawn the second shortest straw, it was up to him to take the mail."

His horse was getting restless. Billy had waited so long for the dignitaries to finish their speeches and ceremonies, he was nervous now too. Finally, William H. Russell and Alexander Majors handed over the mailbag and Billy quickly tossed it onto his saddle. Instantly his foot hit the stirrup and he was mounted. A cannon fired, the crowd hollered. As he dashed out of the stables, people tried to snatch tufts of the horse's tail as keepsakes. The *St. Joseph Weekly West* newspaper headlines recorded the whole event: "Horse and rider started off amid the loud and

Pony Express rider galloping by men stringing telegraph wires LIBRARY OF CONGRESS PRINTS AND PHOTOGRAPHS DIVISION, WOOD ENGRAVING PHOTOGRAPHED BY SAVAGE, SALT LAKE CITY, 1867; FROM A PAINTING BY GEORGE M. OTTINGER.

continuous cheers of the assembled multitude, all anxious to witness every particular of the inauguration of this greatest enterprise."

Today we remember the Pony Express as a bold endeavor, born from a necessity of the times. Before 1860 it took over a month, one way, for anyone to receive messages east to west. At the time, the stage and freight company of Russell, Majors and Waddell operated one of the major stage lines. The owners understood that people out West wanted a better way to receive information from across the country. This new idea of a faster mail relay service using horses, relay riders, and stations meant that people out in the gold mines of California could receive information, amazingly, in only ten days.

Like Billy, all the XP riders knew they were faced with a job that took energy and grit from both themselves and their horses. These young men, all from fourteen to eighteen years old, swore an oath to the Russell, Majors and Waddell company to carry out their relays the best they could. They would ride nonstop, day and night, no matter the weather. The mail had to be carried as quickly as possible, but this was a route of almost two thousand miles. Its terrain changed almost as often as the weather, from rolling prairies and rushing rivers to dry desert alkali and high mountain passes. Even with the additional stations the stage company had built along the route, the trail would be dangerous. Billy had signed his contract knowing there would be risk and rough riding. He also knew he'd be paid the whopping sum of almost one hundred dollars a month, well worth all he'd have to endure. It was reassuring to know that he'd also be riding a top-quality horse. Spread throughout the 150-plus relay stations were over five hundred horses, all grain fed and specially chosen for their stamina and temperament. The horses on the east side of the route were like Billy's, having mainly thoroughbred bloodlines. Those out West had mustang heritage and were known for their toughness and speed. All the animals were picked to fit the terrain they would be ridden across.

When Billy signed up to ride, he was impressed by a special piece of equipment designed to safely and quickly relay the mail from horse to horse. The mailbag, called a mochila, was a large leather square made to fit over the entire top of a small lightweight saddle. To carry the letters, four locked pockets were attached to each of the mochila's lower corners, and the whole thing was oiled to protect its contents from rivers, rain, or snow. Holes were cut into the top of the mochila for the saddle horn and cantle of the saddle to poke through. This helped keep the mailbag securely centered on the saddle while horse and rider sped along.

Although the relay riders got most of the glory, it was the station keepers who kept the Pony Express going. These tough men had to be both horse wranglers and caretakers. They tended not only to the horses' needs but also to those of the riders. Hay and grain had to be freighted in to keep the stations running, as well as food for the riders. As Billy learned while out on the trail, there were two types of stations. The first was designated a "relay stop," where a rider quickly relayed the mochila, changed mounts, and continued on. The other was known as a "home station," where a new rider would take over the relay. This station was also where the boys slept and ate before catching their next relay. If a rider had ridden in from the West, he would wait for the next relay coming in from the East and then ride his own route again, but in reverse. Because the horsemen, including Billy, rode the same trails back and forth, riders and horses came to know their areas extremely well. If a storm swelled a river, or a snowstorm covered the landscape, horse and rider kept the mail running on time because they knew the terrain. Unlike these fast-moving riders, though, it was the station keepers who had the most dangerous job. They had to stay in one place at the station, and in spite of the fact that most stations were built of rock, logs, or adobe, many were burned to the ground during Indian uprisings in Utah and other parts of the West. Even with well-defended buildings, horses were stolen, and several station keepers died.

As the light was fading that April night, Billy rode his horse through the St. Joe crowds and down the cobblestone street to the Missouri River. He had heard the ferryboat *Denver* blow its horn and knew it was waiting at the landing for him—the first XP rider leaving from the East. Under a full head of steam, it ferried him and his horse to the Kansas side of the river, where

Billy continued his relay westward. He smiled to himself, knowing that another rider out of California was headed toward St. Joseph at that very moment, and, somewhere out on the trail, the XP riders would cross paths. Records say that each rider was to travel seventy to one hundred miles a day, exchanging horses every ten to fifteen miles, depending on the terrain. The route was a ride of nearly two thousand miles one way, so there was no time to waste anywhere. Billy knew that the only delay the company approved was when a rider arrived at the station for the mail exchange. Here the next horse and rider were to be ready. The mochila was thrown onto the waiting, saddled horse, and, with a gallant leap, the rider mounted and swiftly continued down the trail—all within only two minutes. Billy had practiced mounting his horse for days before the start and had mastered a speedy mount, well under the two-minute timetable.

Although sometimes he rode with a bit of wildness, Billy completed his relays as swiftly as he could. Often, he got to wondering what letters he might be carrying. He'd heard it was expensive to send a letter by Pony Express, costing five dollars for each half-ounce of mail. That was a mighty large sum in 1860. Most of the correspondences at first were business letters demanding rapid transport across the country. Because this mail would be carried on horseback, each letter had to be written on pieces of paper that were small and as thin as tissue. This kept down the weight and allowed a larger number of letters to be transported. Before they were packed into the mochila pockets, the letters were bundled and carefully wrapped in oil silk, as waterproofing from the elements. Whether traveling east or west, all the mail was securely locked inside the mochila pockets, and the mailbag wouldn't be opened again until it reached its final destination, either in St. Joseph, Missouri, or Sacramento, California. One Missouri newspaper reporter wrote, "It's a mighty far piece to California, with many a dangerous twist and turn for so small a parcel . . . but what an exhilarating feat!"

During the short span of its operation—only eighteen months—the Pony Express delivered almost thirty-five thousand letters between Missouri and California. Billy would never forget one record-making relay that he and his fellow XP riders took part in. On November 7, 1860, the boys carried word of Abraham Lincoln's election as president. They rode the route in only seven days. This is still considered one of the most significant accomplishments of the Central Overland Pony Express.

But by February of 1861, talk of a civil war between the northern and southern states was drifting across the country. At the same time, telegraph lines were expanding westward. This new technology put the mail-relay business of Russell, Majors and Waddell in peril. More change was on the way. On April 12, 1861, the Civil War began and plunged the country into chaos. In the midst of war, though, telegraph lines continued to spread across the nation. On October 24, the transcontinental telegraph reached Salt Lake City, and two days later, the final wire connection was made between East and West. This meant that mail relays on horseback were no longer needed. They had become obsolete. The dream and excitement of the Central Overland Pony Express were over, and Billy Richardson was out of a job.

During his whole term of employment, Billy had relayed mail in true Pony Express style and spirit. Through rain and snow, ink-black nights, or wild winds and scorching sun, Billy fulfilled his contract. We can only imagine how many times he made swift arrivals at relay stations. What a sight he must have made, galloping into a station, tossing his leg over quickly to dismount, his boots hitting the ground almost before his horse had stopped. How many mail-filled mochilas had he swapped onto a waiting horse, swinging up into the saddle to leave only dust or mud in his wake? We shall never truly know. It's lost to legend now.

Rumor has it that after a few years, Billy moved on to Fort Laramie in the Nebraska Territory (present-day Wyoming) to live with his sister. It was here they say that Billy caught pneumonia and, unable to recover, died. He was all of twenty-eight years old. He is said to be buried in the Old Fort Laramie Cemetery. Little did he or anyone who worked for the Pony Express think that their amazing endeavor would create a lasting legacy that would mark America's history forever.

Today the heritage and spirit of the Pony Express are still celebrated each June. Since 1977, members of the National Pony Express Association (NPEA) have recreated an XP relay, carrying US mail. Over five hundred men and women of this nonprofit, volunteer organization ride a non-stop relay for ten days, much as it was done in 1860. Anyone is welcome to send a letter during the June event, and every piece of mail receives commemorative postal cancellations stating that it was carried by Pony Express. The ride starts either from the Patee House in St. Joseph, Missouri (the original XP headquarters), or from Old Sacramento in California. The starting point alternates every other year. A mochila, styled after the same type Billy used, carries the commemorative mail. Traveling day and night, the riders exchange the mochila at designated relay stops every two to five miles, following as much of the original trail as possible. Although most of the route is now lost amid the US interstate highway system, you can still see traces of stations and trail ruts scattered across the eight states that the trail crosses. Markers can be found in Missouri, Kansas, Nebraska, Colorado, Wyoming, Utah, Nevada, and California. In 1992, thanks to the help of the NPEA and the National Forest Service and other government agencies, Congress designated this route as the Pony Express National Historic Trail.

In 1996, members of the NPEA were honored to be chosen to take part in another historic event. XP riders would relay the Olympic torch 365 miles across Nebraska, as part of the torch's trek from Greece to Atlanta, Georgia, for the opening of the Centennial Olympic Games. This is the only time the Olympic torch has been carried on horseback across America, and in true Pony Express relay style!

Storytellers shall always remember the unbelievable dream of a mail relay that crisscrossed the country and the swift horses and young riders who made the dream come true. Forever woven into the fabric of the American spirit, the story is a fitting legacy for XP riders like Billy. They changed our history, one horse-relayed letter at a time.

Note: There has always been a debate whether it was Johnny Frye or Billy Richardson who was the first rider out of St. Joseph. Either way, the events remain the same.

Plague of locusts attacking a field GETTY IMAGES/IVAN-96

Grasshoppers for Supper

Candace Simar

Seven-year-old Laura Ingalls noticed a dark cloud churning in the western sky during the summer of 1873 in Walnut Grove, Minnesota. It wasn't a prairie fire roaring toward them. Strange reflections showed within the swirling mass. The cloud chattered like a speeding locomotive. It looked like a twister or a summer storm.

Laura describes what happened next in her book *On the Banks of Plum Creek*. "The cloud was grasshoppers. Their bodies hid the sun and made darkness. Their large, thin wings gleamed and glittered. The rasping whirring of their wings filled the whole air and they hit the ground and the house with the noise of a hailstorm. . . ."

Some feared the end of the world had come when trillions of Rocky Mountain locusts dropped from the sky like a summer blizzard. They fell on fields, gardens, streams, farm buildings, animals, and houses like a ravenous beast. The sounds of crunching, scratching, and grinding jaws made it impossible for the settlers to converse without shouting. The insects slammed against buildings and trees like hail, pounding and drumming.

People ran for cover. Those caught out in the open found themselves disoriented in a swirling swarm of wings and legs. The locusts tangled in people's hair and left lacerations with their sharp wings, especially around the eyes and face. They flew into open mouths and climbed into nostrils and ears. Their sharp wings cut into bare feet. Dogs howled as the grasshoppers crawled into their eyes and ears. Cattle stampeded. Every person and animal sought shelter. Family members banged pans or blew horns to help loved ones find their way back to shelter through the hideous, roaring swarm.

The Rocky Mountain locusts were smaller than most grasshoppers, only one and a half inches long. They crept inside houses through open windows, cracks under doors, and down chimneys. Women and children swept them up and burned them in the stove, causing an acrid stench that stung their eyes and made settlers' small huts as hot as ovens. Helpless farmers watched through their windows as the locusts devoured every blade of prairie grass, every stem of wheat, and every plant in fields and gardens.

Some farmers rushed to set smudge fires around their fields, hoping to drive the grasshoppers away with smoke. They raked the insects into huge piles and lit them on fire, but it was like a drop in the bucket. The farmers couldn't keep up. The hordes of hoppers were everywhere, reportedly stacked up three inches deep in places, devouring one man's sixty-acre wheat crop in less than an hour.

People covered their wells to protect their water supply. Women draped plants with quilts in a futile attempt to spare their gardens. Others fired guns or banged on metal pans in an effort to frighten the locusts away. Some started prairie fires or burned entire fields.

The hoppers ignored the sounds of banging pans. They were not dislodged by smudge fires. They chewed the quilts spread over the tomato plants and any clothes left hanging on the clothesline. They consumed every blade of grass and every blooming flower. They clogged rivers and streams. In western Minnesota they ate an entire field of onions, leaving only a strong odor and empty indentations where the onions had nestled in the soil. They gnawed the sweaty salt from hoe and rake handles. The hoppers left nothing green.

Only the chickens were fat and satisfied, but their eggs carried an unpleasant flavor and were tinted an unusual color.

When the hoppers had eaten everything there was to be eaten, they deposited trillions of eggs across the denuded terrain. Only then did they swarm, rise skyward, and fly off to destroy another place.

Farmers living on the northern edges of the infestation believed the eggs could not possibly survive the frigid winters of Dakota Territory, Minnesota, or Canada. It wouldn't happen again, they comforted one another. These farmers tightened their belts and vowed to plant again the following year. Farmers were familiar with hardships and knew how to squeak by in a lean year. They sold their stock because they lacked fodder to feed them through the winter. They dipped into what little savings they had. They vowed to survive.

In February, a Minnesota farmer dug up a square inch of frozen soil from his field and left it overnight on his kitchen table to thaw. By morning, 150 grasshopper larvae wiggled on his table. At that rate, he calculated 940,896,000 Rocky Mountain locusts would hatch per acre on his farm. In total, 6,586,272,000 Rocky Mountain locusts could be expected in one seven-acre field. He quipped, "From present prospects the hoppers will be right smart, powerful hungry and will do a heap of damage."

The Rocky Mountain locusts hatched the following spring, just as the wheat was about two inches high. The locust hatchlings could not fly for the first five to seven weeks. They crawled across the landscape in huge armies, some forty miles wide and up to one hundred miles long. The grasshoppers left behind a savaged landscape, akin to bleak winter rather than green summer.

People tied strings around the bottoms of their pant legs and at the cuffs of their sleeves to keep the locusts from crawling inside their clothing. Many wore veils to keep the insects out of their faces.

One man said, "The grasshoppers are making a clean sweep of the grain and shrubbery of all kinds, and are not leaving a living thing on improved lands." When the grasshoppers became old enough to lay eggs, they did so by the trillions and flew away to begin the vicious cycle again. Grasshopper infestations continued for five years.

There were no insecticides to help the farmers get rid of the Rocky Mountain locusts. For the first time in the history of the United States, farmers could not feed their families. Government subsidies were instituted.

Desperate farmers invented killing machines called "hopperdozers." These dozers were sheets of metal smeared with coal tar or molasses. Two people, or one person plus a horse, dragged the dozer through the fields. The grasshoppers caught in the sticky substance on the metal. The captured hoppers were scraped into a fire at the end of each row. Even long hours in the field did not diminish the number of Rocky Mountain locusts. They were too numerous.

County fairs were cancelled because farmers had no produce to exhibit. Trains stopped running on tracks made slippery by crushed hoppers. Throughout the region, flour mills shut their doors because they had no wheat to mill. With their savings used up, the settlers were close to starvation.

Many settlers gave up and returned east, leaving their hard-won farms and ranches for jobs in factories or sawmills. The Rocky Mountain locusts attacked only open prairies, and there was work available for displaced farmers in wooded areas of the country. Some covered wagons heading east bore painted grasshoppers on their canvas covers, with the words, "He won."

Extermination attempts failed, despite creative efforts to gather and destroy the invaders. Some counties required every male between the ages of twenty-one and sixty (excluding "paupers, idiots, and lunatics") in the infected areas to devote one day a week for five weeks to killing young grasshoppers and eggs. Local governments paid a bounty of up to $2.50 per bushel for grasshoppers or fifty cents a gallon for eggs. Most townships paid less.

A four-year-old Minnesota boy earned enough money to buy a two-dollar pair of shoes by gathering grasshoppers for three cents a bushel.

The bounty, in many cases, became the settlers' entire annual income. Farmers had nothing to harvest and nothing to sell. Bank notes remained unpaid. Larders stood empty. One family survived on the bark of slippery elm and rutabagas. In desperation, many turned to the invader itself for sustenance.

Plains Indians had long considered the Rocky Mountain locust a staple in their diet. Native Americans ate them pounded into flour or boiled in stews and found them high in protein, energy, and fat.

Starving settlers roasted hoppers over open fires, stirred them into stews and soups, and crushed them into a paste that they then dried into flour for baking. They ate them fried, dousing the delicacy with salt, pepper, and vinegar. Grasshoppers had a distinctive odor that disappeared after cooking. Some said they tasted like crawfish, but all agreed—Rocky Mountain locusts tasted best with their sharp wings and legs removed.

C. V. Ross, a Missouri entomologist, presented a paper on his experiences with Rocky Mountain locusts as a food. He is quoted as saying, "I found the chitinous covering and the corneous parts—especially the spines of the tibia—dry and chippy, and somewhat irritating to the throat. This objection would not apply, with the same force, to the mature individuals, especially of larger species, where the heads, legs, and wings are carefully separated before cooking. In fact, some of the mature insects prepared in this way, then boiled and afterward stewed with a few vegetables, and a little butter, pepper, salt and vinegar, made an excellent fricassee."

The Rocky Mountain locusts invaded the center of North America from Alberta, Canada, to Dallas, Texas, spreading like a huge teardrop across the center of the continent. The largest swarm is believed to have happened in 1875, when the swarm was estimated to contain several trillion locusts. It was the largest cloud in the history of the world and was thought to weigh several million tons.

The area affected by the Rocky Mountain locusts equaled the combined areas of Connecticut, Delaware, Maine, Maryland, Massachusetts, New Hampshire, New Jersey, New York, Pennsylvania, Rhode Island, and Vermont. Prairie states directly affected by the locusts included Minnesota, Iowa, Colorado, Kansas, Nebraska, Missouri, Texas, and the Dakota Territory—a region of 198,000 square miles covered with trillions of insects.

The *Smithsonian* magazine named the Rocky Mountain locusts and the carrier pigeons as the two largest groups of animals in the history of the world.

An itinerant priest serving in Dakota Territory shared a prayer he had written.

You may find it inscribed on a museum wall at Fort Sisseton, South Dakota:

I bid you depart, animals of destruction. Leave our fields and plains immediately. Live no longer in them but pass over into places where you can harm no one. I call God's wrath upon you, and diminishing from day to day, may you disappear except where you serve the health and good purposes of mankind. May no trace of you be found. Amen.

Midwestern states were on the brink of bankruptcy. Minnesota Governor Pillsbury called for a day of prayer and fasting on April 26, 1877, in a desperate attempt to eradicate the Rocky Mountain locust. Newspaper articles ridiculed the governor and named him "superstitious," but government offices and businesses closed as people gathered in city halls, schools, and churches to pray for relief from the scourge of the hoppers. A few days later, a dramatic late spring snowstorm fell upon the Midwest.

That same year, a miracle happened. The grasshoppers flew away without depositing their eggs. Farmers reported, "little, dark whirlwinds here and there which after a while formed into dark clouds, leaving in the same way they had come."

Dead grasshoppers were seen floating an inch and a half deep over Lake Superior. Officials noticed red spots under their wings, but otherwise the dead locusts appeared normal.

A woman in Boston wrote a letter to her sister in Minnesota saying that she "knew where the grasshoppers had gone." She had been hanging laundry in her yard when a "strange, chattering cloud flew overhead. A few grasshoppers dropped into her clothes basket. She watched as the cloud flew out over the Atlantic Ocean." This woman's letter can be seen in the Minnesota History Center in Saint Paul, Minnesota.

What happened? Was it divine intervention? Whatever the reason, the Rocky Mountain locusts have been extinct ever since. One specimen remains in the Smithsonian Museum in Washington, DC. Scientists report that Rocky Mountain locusts can sometimes be found frozen in glaciers.

In 1877, without the destructive insects, Minnesota yielded the biggest wheat crop that the state had ever known. Farmers prospered once again. Trains hauled wheat to market unhindered. Flour mills ground enough wheat to feed America and sell to other countries.

The hardship and suffering caused by the Rocky Mountain locusts faded among the lost pages of history.

Grasshopper suppers became part of pioneer legend.

Howdy, Pilgrim: Quakers in Wild West Texas

S. J. Dahlstrom

Something was bugging Paris Cox. He couldn't put his finger on it, but every night when the sun went down in Boxley, Indiana, he wondered what was over that burning horizon.

His sawmill was humming every day, out of necessity. By now, in 1876, the Civil War had been over for a decade, and Indiana was no longer a frontier. People were flooding into the state and swelling the town of Indianapolis, just thirty miles to the south. Settlers were clearing the thick hardwood forests, sawing timber for homes and businesses, planting crops, and turning Indiana into a breadbasket for the nation. Paris had a young wife, a thriving vocation, and most importantly, he knew who he was in the universe. He was a Quaker.

Quakers, or the Society of Friends, hadn't fought in the Civil War. They were pacifists and believed that all conflicts could have a nonviolent solution if people would see God in one another. During the recent war, at least 620,000 fellow Americans had died; 24,000 had been killed from Indiana alone. This meant that 35 percent of the Hoosiers, or citizens of Indiana, who had gone to the war had perished. Paris had stayed home, having bought a legal exemption from service.

This fact must not have made any friends for Paris or other Quakers.

So, maybe despite Paris Cox's comfortable financial situation, it was no surprise that when a land agent appeared in his small town selling land in Texas, Paris listened. He listened closely, and then bought a small piece of that wild prairie—sight unseen. One wonders what his wife must have said. Texas was another world.

Committed in his mind to doing something besides run a sawmill for the rest of his life, Paris attached himself the next year to a party of buffalo hunters. He bought a rifle, a famed .50 caliber Sharps. Buffalo hunting was not a usual occupation for a Quaker, to say the least. Paris undoubtedly asked the blessing of the congregation's elders, and so equipped, he headed out to the frontier with men with whom he must have shared little in common.

The party hunted and explored all the way to the Pecos River in New Mexico. Whether or not he told his new companions he was home hunting along the way, curious about the bit

Quakers stand outside of the meetinghouse they built in Maryetta in the late 1880s SOUTHWEST COLLECTION/ TEXAS TECH UNIVERSITY

of prairie he already owned, we don't know. It is recorded that when he was on the flat Llano Estacado of West Texas, he said, "Here by the will of God will be my home."

THE FIRST YEAR
Whatever Paris was looking for, he had found it on land no one else was interested in. The Llano was a region 250 miles by 150 miles where no white men had ever lived. New Mexican settlement had stopped on the Llano's western edge, and Texan settlement had been beaten back by the Comanches on the eastern. The closest town to that western edge was Colorado City, 120 miles toward Fort Worth.

Indians didn't spend much time in the Llano either. The region was merely their escape route when the cavalry came too close to their stronghold in Palo Duro Canyon. For hundreds of miles in every direction, the area was known as the Comancheria. The same year that Paris was picking out real estate, US Army Captain Nicholas Nolan famously led his troop of Buffalo Soldiers on a quest, trailing Comanches. Five men and all the troop's horses died of thirst in what was called "The Staked Plains Horror." Years later, author Elmer Kelton fictionalized this awful tale in his novel, *The Wolf and the Buffalo*.

This was the same piece of land that another army officer, Randolph Marcy, wrote of in 1849, calling it "the dreaded Llano Estacado ... the Zahara [Sahara] of North America." Marcy went on to describe its prospects: "It is a region almost as vast and as trackless as the ocean—a land where no man either savage or civilized permanently abides; it spreads forth into a treeless, desolate waste of uninhabitable solitude, which has always been and must continue, uninhabited forever."

Early authors seemed to have had a competition over who could write the most foreboding prose about the area. The famous soldier and explorer Albert Pike detailed the Llano in almost poetic fashion: "Not a tree, nor a bush, not a shrub, not a tall weed lifts its head above the barren grandeur of the desert ... not a stone ... nothing."

But Paris had undoubtedly never read any Marcy or Pike books, or Nolan dispatches from the field. How strange that the same piece of land had struck him so utterly the opposite. The fact that Paris deliberately chose to settle in an area so ill-spoken of shows either an outrageous naivete, or, in like manner, courage.

While Nolan's men, driven wild by thirst, were deserting their command that same year to the south, Paris and his band of buffalo hunters must have hit the spring rains perfectly. The cool showers would have made the deep Llano topsoil practically spongy beneath young Paris's feet. The lack of running water was no problem—there were freshwater lakes every five miles. Paris learned that these were called playas. There were still plenty of buffalo, and herds of antelope grazed through the vast wildflower bloom of red and yellow Indian blankets and oceans of purple prairie verbena and horsemint.

Paris must have heard that the dreaded Comanches had been whipped by Colonel Ranald Mackenzie in Palo Duro Canyon three years before. A young rancher, Charles Goodnight, was now taking cattle into that heart of the former Comanche empire. Cattlemen and Comanches knew enough to stay in the lowlands, or rolling plains, east of the Llano, where there was water and wood and protection from the elements.

And the best part was, there was no timber or brush to clear. These naked plains were where Paris would settle. As a sawmill man, he surely considered this loss of his developed expertise, but it was the easy pickings for farming that must have sold him. He had not yet discovered the mysterious character of the Llano. It was a land that couldn't be trusted.

Paris decided to establish a whole town and picked a spot that adjoined the property he had bought. The town site overlooked a large fifty-acre playa. Small hills rose on either side, offering a view of a flat earth, bending toward the horizon. Paris then returned home, petitioned his church, and bought the additional fifty thousand acres he wanted for his town. He had his solitude. Now he would make it habitable.

He wrote up a large handbill to advertise his settlement. He would sell the land for fifty cents an acre. He invested in a four-thousand-dollar well for the town and offered to have any land plowed up at no extra expense. He also hired a well digger to put in a test garden.

The handbill read "THE GOLDEN OPPORTUNITY OF OUR LIVES," and described the country as "an exceedingly healthy locality and excellent water." The water, he explained, was not running water but came from the pools that formed on every section of land. "It seems nature has arranged them for drainage, and to hold creek water. It is believed that almost all of them might be made to hold creek water all the year."

Paris's belief was yet to be proven.

He was no charlatan, however, and his other observations were made with sincere honesty. He detailed the rattlesnakes—"but not near so many as we expected to find"—and the tarantulas, centipedes, and grasshoppers. He said that the Indians were all but gone, and that "Texas was no longer a place of resort for thieves and robbers."

The "kind of men wanted" did not have to be exclusively Quaker. Paris must have known he needed warm bodies to help him. Still, he listed the qualifications as "good, honest, moral, religious, and temperance . . . but also men of courage and energy; men who are willing to undergo the privations and hardships of a new country for the sake of a home of their own."

Back home Paris had three takers. So, in October of 1879, his own and the three other families left the comforts of rural Indiana and headed west.

Nothing of the trip is recorded. If Paris felt any anxiety, he didn't say, but his pioneer comrades must have started wondering why they kept going west day after day into the bleak unknown. Heading into winter at the end of an eleven-hundred-mile wagon trip, the four men and their women and children finally unloaded their wagons into a sea of grass. They could hardly have picked a worse time to begin homesteading a barren land.

Paris named the town Maryetta, after his wife. Perhaps this was to soften some of the doubt and fear that must have been percolating in her mind, along with the fact that the couple had two small boys now. Whatever their private conversations must have been, the four families went to work preparing for their first plains winter.

Paris built a dugout. This was a sod house partially dug into the prairie clay. He must have seen these throughout his travels in the West and known that freighting in wood from Colorado City was not an option that late in the year. Strangely, the other three families did not follow suit and were content to winter in canvas tents. They were about to discover why tents were a bad idea.

Paris's handbills had never mentioned the wind, perhaps because their author had never spent more than a few months of a rainy springtime in the country. Paris had reported that Llano winters could still be cold, although not nearly as cold as Indiana's and certainly with less snow. But he had misread these details because he was uninformed about the terrifying effects of cold-season winds. The Llano was 3,200 feet above sea level. And although it had an average January low temperature of twenty-six degrees, the wind chill from a pretty standard fifty-mile-per-hour gale was close to zero.

Arriving in winter also meant that there just wasn't much the settlers could do to improve their situation. They couldn't clear land, gather wood, turn over sod, or plant crops. They had no lumber for construction. The men must have spent hours hunting for game, while the women sat and listened to the canvas snap and pop in the wind. One particularly strong wind blew several of the tents away when the men were gone. Pieces of the canvas ended up in Blanco Canyon, over twenty miles away.

Still, that first year they had a Christmas tree. It was a cedar retrieved from twenty-five miles to the east.

It cannot be understated how difficult this new set of circumstances must have been to people used to the forested confines of the fertile lands of America's Mississippi River basin. Unending sky and wind and misery were their new community.

So, it was no surprise that in May 1880, Paris and his wife watched the three other families load their wagons and return East. The golden opportunity of their lives was not to be.

SLOW SUCCESS

Paris didn't keep a journal, so no one knows what thoughts drifted through his head that lonely year of 1880. He must have had doubts. Along with being a dreamer, he must have been a poet and philosopher to be able to turn the disaster of the first year into something worth salvaging. Perhaps the Bible he knew so well gave him vision and courage: "And he shall be like the tree planted by rivers of water that bringeth forth his fruit in his season, and his leaf shall not wither, and whatsoever he doeth shall prosper."

His wife must have been of as sturdy a stock as he was. Hands rubbed raw from hauling water and doing laundry and preparing meals and sweeping dirt floors, she stood beside her husband in a wilderness that thousands of years had bluntly said to humans, "Stay out."

Whatever had bugged Paris about life in the East, it still outweighed the "privations and hardships" he was experiencing. The man didn't flinch.

He wrote more letters and handbills, and by the next year he had recruited ten families, including his parents and brother. He even enlisted a doctor. The fresh pioneers showed up in the spring of 1881 and met a more seasoned Paris, one who knew a bit more of the secrets of life on the Llano.

By 1882, the ten families had successfully grown corn, oats, and sorghum. They also harvested all manner of garden vegetables, such as melons, pumpkins, and potatoes. Ignoring the ideas of cattlemen, they went into small-scale stock farming, raising pigs, cows, and sheep. Things were looking up. Paris hand-dug an eighty-two-foot well. The trial of that achievement is almost beyond imagination. The man had grit.

There is a record of a Quaker, or Friends, meeting held during this time. ("Meeting" was the Quakers' name for church services.) These meetings were characterized by "waiting on God" and had a decided lack of formality, except for the tradition of hand shaking. These pioneer Quakers met three times a week, twice on their strictly observed Sunday Sabbath. They reported back to their community in Indiana that there had been no cases of "transgression of discipline," that there were no poor needing assistance, that each family had a Bible and read it daily, that there was no manufacture or traffic in intoxicating liquors, and that—perhaps humorously—"Our members are free from the habitual use of tobacco, except one."

One old tobacco chewer on the plains wasn't going to have anyone tell him he couldn't have a dip. One wonders what the definition of "habitual" might have entailed.

A little boy named J. W. Hunt was raised in Estacado during the bountiful seven-year period that lasted from 1881 to 1888 (the US post office had made the town change its name to Estacado when another town called Maryetta was discovered in South Texas). Later, J. W. Hunt wrote fondly of his early experiences. "Boys were not just boys. They were men. They had to be." These Estacado pioneer boys roped mustangs and broke them and shot bear and antelope. Surprisingly, recreation arrived on the plains too. Estacado competed with the town of Plainview for baseball bragging rights, beating Plainview once, 42–12, in a game lasting all day.

Soon the town built a school and a courthouse, and numerous merchants filled in the gaps. Lumber was hauled from Amarillo and Colorado City. Windmills provided relief from the unreliable playas and the never-ending process of hauling water up from the city well. Buffalo still made occasional appearances, and Paris provided the town with their hides and meat with his old Sharps.

Tragedy finally struck in 1885. Paris's niece, five-year-old Bertha Cox, was bitten by a rattlesnake and died. She was the first white settler to die on the Llano. They buried her in a plot that they had set aside for the town's cemetery, five years before. Many must have wondered at this sad occasion, "Was all this worth it?"

BIRTH OF A GHOST TOWN

Then Estacado went into decline, as quickly and painfully as it had been birthed. The details are buried with the man, but Paris died of throat cancer in 1888. How long he struggled or what treatments he endured are facts left unwritten. His vision and leadership could not be replaced.

Paris's brother and father stayed on, and in 1890 even founded a college, the Central Plains Academy. The town reached its peak population of 238 that same year.

But bad luck followed in waves, sealing the town's destiny. The most decisive turn happened when the fickle nature of the Llano finally caught up with the small town. A four-year drought turned the lush playa lakes into miniature dust bowls. The crops withered in the dry winds of spring and summer, and wildfire haunted every evening.

The town lost its status as the county seat of Crosby when the prairie was finally surveyed and organized. Estacado was found to be in the county of Lubbock, not Crosby. A more centralized town was chosen, and with it went businesses and government money.

The Quakers also bristled at clashes with the predominant culture of the plains—big ranches and their cowboys. Cowboys wanted saloons and women, and the pretty Quaker girls were their most convenient option for the latter. And the ranchers didn't like seeing rangeland plowed up for crops—crops that usually didn't survive the high and dry climate.

So, in 1893 the Friends made the hard decision to leave. The college closed, and most of the townspeople moved to another more prosperous Friends community in Houston.

The pluck and inherent conflicts of Paris Cox's vision told a good story—a story that Hollywood noticed. In the 1947 John Wayne Western *Angel and the Badman*, "Duke" plays the gunslinger Quirt Evans. Quirt is injured and then rescued by a family of Pennsylvania Quakers who had just moved out to the fringes of the Texas frontier. The family doctor makes a perceptive speech to the naive Quakers:

"This isn't civilized Pennsylvania . . . this is raw frontier. You must take a realistic attitude. This is a place where mayhem, theft, and murder are the common place instead of the unusual."

John Wayne, perhaps most famously known for the line "Howdy, Pilgrim," implying that he was greeting ignorant newcomers, has this exchange with his pretty and young Quaker love interest:

"Are there very many of you Quakers?"

"Very few," she replies.

"Sorta figured that," he responds dryly.

Of course, the legacy of Estacado isn't that simple or one-sided. Someone had to pack up and crack the country open. Paris might be proud to know that the Llano is now a cornucopia of agriculture, thanks to the modern technology of deep irrigation wells that draw water from the immense Ogallala Aquifer that underlies the Llano. The region now produces more cotton per capita than any area in the world, not to mention other cash crops. Paris wasn't all wrong.

One wonders what pushes men like Paris away from comforts and into certain hardship, and to do it all through labor and not conquest—the Quaker way. He wrote, "This is an opening . . . to become independent in the world, almost unexcelled." Like most founding fathers, he only got a glimpse of that treasured independence.

For men like Paris, that was enough.

Coal for Supper

Nancy Oswald

Would you travel more than seven thousand miles from your home to start a new life? Would you leave behind everything you loved—your friends, your community, your house, and belongings? Would you move to a place where you had to walk eight miles for supplies and food to cook with? That's exactly what eleven-year-old Reuben Grupitzky did in the spring of 1882, when he moved with his family from Russia to a remote area of Colorado.

Life had become unbearable for Jews in Russia. In May of 1881, harsh anti-Jewish laws had been put in place by the new Russian leader, Tsar Alexander III. These laws kept Jews from owning land and forced them to live in separate communities. If Jews were caught outside of their *shtetyl*, or ghetto, they would be punished and expelled from Russia without having a chance to defend themselves. Reuben's family, like all Russian Jewish families, also had to follow strict rules about when and where they could do business. All over Russia, anti-Jewish rioting occurred. Angry mobs carrying sticks and throwing stones attacked homes and destroyed property and Jewish businesses. If Reuben had been a teen, he would have been forced to enlist in the Tsar's army.

Reuben's family decided it was time to leave. His father, a widower, packed quickly, taking only what family members could carry. The Grupitzkys planned to join a group of Russian Jews heading for America, where they could farm and own land. The group planned to live together in an agricultural colony.

When Reuben and his family reached New York City, the Hebrew Immigration Society helped the colonists find a new home. The society had been in contact with a miner and businessman from Cotopaxi, Colorado, named Emanuel Saltiel. Saltiel promised to supply the colonists with land, houses, barns, and enough farming equipment and supplies to make a fresh start.

Reuben's family was among the first fifty colonists to head west. They boarded a train in New York City, leaving behind the noise and bustle of the crowded eastern cities. The train clattered, bumped, and swayed across the Great Plains. Miles of empty space—vast areas where no one lived—separated the few large towns they passed through.

THE VETA PASS.

Vintage engraving of steam train going through the La Veta Pass, Colorado, nineteenth century GETTY IMAGES/
DUNCAN1890

In Pueblo, Colorado, Reuben and the other colonists changed trains and traveled toward the mountains. Their train wove through twisty, narrow gorges and between steep, rocky cliffs where there were no roads. In some places, the white-capped rapids of the Arkansas River nearly touched the tracks. Reuben must have wondered if he'd be lost forever in the winding river canyon.

Finally, the colonists reached the small town of Cotopaxi, at the north end of the Sangre de Cristo Mountains. All of the buildings—a hotel and store, a blacksmith shop, a meetinghouse, and a few scattered houses and huts—could be counted on fingers and toes. Reuben and the others were greeted by a group of local people—ranchers and cowboys—wearing jeans and dusty hats. They had shown up at the train station like looky-loos at a circus sideshow, just to watch the arrival of the oddly dressed outsiders. Many of the locals were openly rude.

A few sympathetic onlookers later described the "looks of terror and awe" on the colonists' faces as they stepped off the train. Farther along the tracks, a huge water tank towered above the rails. It was used to refill the boilers for the steam engines before the trains continued west between the steep red cliffs that lined the way upriver to the small town of Salida and points beyond. Soon the train whistle blew, and the echoes from the locomotive faded into the distance, leaving Reuben and the others standing by the railroad station with the few personal belongings they had been able to bring with them from Russia.

A total of fifty men, women, and children arrived in Cotopaxi on May 8, 1882. During the summer, five more families came, almost doubling the population of the small town. Before leaving New York City, the colonists had been told everything would be ready for them when they arrived. They spoke no English, so conversations in America had to be translated from Yiddish, the language they had spoken in Russia, to English and back again to Yiddish. That's how Reuben's father learned that most of the houses that had been promised to them were located four to eight miles away from town, and that of the twenty houses promised, only twelve of them were finished. None of the houses had windows or doors, and only four of the houses had stoves, but no chimneys to vent the smoke.

The Jewish people turned to Emanuel Saltiel, the miner and businessman, for an explanation. He told the colonists that workmen were hard to find. The windows and doors had been sent for in Denver, but the order had been delayed. Saltiel had also agreed to supply farming equipment and seed, but only two plows and one team of horses were available.

Saltiel housed the newcomers in the hotel and went on a business trip, leaving the colonists to manage on their own. They decided to live in the half-finished houses, so they could get their crops planted. The colonists borrowed plows, horses, and other equipment from the owner of the local store, A. S. Hart, a cousin and partner to Saltiel. Credit was allowed for the purchase of household supplies, food, and personal items.

The colonists soon found out that the land Saltiel had provided was not farming land. It had no irrigation water and was rocky and difficult to plow. Most of it was at an elevation of more than eight thousand feet at the base of the mountains. It was nearly June before all the crops were planted. One colonist later said, "It was the poorest place in the world for farming, poor land, lots of rocks and no water, and the few crops we were able to raise, by a miracle, were mostly eaten by cattle belonging to the neighboring settlers."

Over time, chimneys were built and the first houses completed. The warmer summer weather lifted everyone's spirits and brought promise for the future. The colonists needed a place to worship, so they found an abandoned cabin in Cotopaxi to use as a synagogue. Two weddings were held during the first summer, and a Sefer Torah—a sacred Jewish scroll—was donated to the colony by an organization in New York. When the Torah arrived, the group celebrated with "singing hymns and dancing."

The Torah was dedicated on June 23, 1882. At 5:30 p.m., the colonists formed a line outside the synagogue—the elders, each holding a lit candle, stood at the front. Behind them, four single men propped up the poles for a canopy, or *chuppah*, that covered the ark holding the handwritten scrolls. Dressed in their best clothing, the women and children stood at the end of the line.

Reuben entered the synagogue with the other colonists. Chanting, singing, and prayers filled the small building. A newspaper, the *New York Jewish Messenger*, reported, "since human eyes beheld the Rocky Mountains, it was the first time the Jewish law was read in their shadow, and accompanied by the roar of the swift Arkansas River."

After the ceremony, Reuben and the others were fed by Mrs. Hart and her daughter in Mrs. Hart's dining room. Mrs. Hart "waited on the poor refugees, whose happy features showed that they will never forget this beautiful day."

The joys of summer ended when an early frost killed the colonists' crops. One man had planted fifteen bags of potatoes, but the potatoes he harvested were smaller than the ones he had planted. Without money from the crops, the colonists had to find work to pay their debts at the store and to provide food and clothing for the winter.

Many of the men took jobs as workers in Saltiel's Cotopaxi mines, walking miles to work for $1.50 a day. They were not paid in cash but paid in vouchers to use in Mr. Hart's store. Others found work with the Denver and Rio Grande Railroad, building track west of Salida. For less than three dollars a day, the men dug trenches, sawed logs, and carried them on their shoulders—three men to a log, down steep slopes—so that later the timber could be shaped into railroad ties.

Reuben's family and the other colonists faced more hardships during the fall and winter. They had to build large bonfires to keep away the "marauding" bears, and after the bears hibernated, starving Ute Indians passed through the area begging for food when the colonists had little to spare. They used up their firewood quickly, and the lack of housing made it necessary for two families to set up camp in canvas tents. Another family spent its first winter in an Indian dugout cave.

More than once, the colonists asked Emanuel Saltiel for help. One of the colonists went to Saltiel, "took him by the hand, and, with tears running down his cheeks, begged him to aid the cold and hungry women and children." Saltiel answered this request with a shrug, refusing to help.

Reuben's father was one of two men who traveled to Denver, 150 miles away, to ask for support from the Jewish community. In return, the Jews in Denver sent two men to Cotopaxi to investigate. In a report written by them and sent to the Hebrew Immigration Society in New York in February 1883, they described the experience of one colonist.

The family of Morris Mimorsky was without food for two days; his wife was sick, and the Arkansas River was swollen to such an extent that it carried destruction in its terrible course. It was a question of life and death. Mimorsky plunged in the stream and, after a desperate effort, in which no other man would venture, reached the opposite shore in safety. He secured the necessary provisions for his sick wife and brought them back with him.

The two men also told others, "We do not exaggerate when we say that a beast could not subsist on these lands."

Some people did not agree that the colonists were suffering. Many spoke out against them. A Denver newspaper, *The Rocky Mountain News*, believed that the difficulties of the Russian Jews were no worse than the hardships of other settlers, saying that "all pioneers must endure some hardship."

Also, a letter from the Hebrew Immigration Society accused the colonists of "begging" instead of spending their own money for what they needed.

Help came from unexpected places. When the train engineers from the Denver and Rio Grande Railroad heard about the Jews' struggles, they tossed extra coal along the tracks when they passed through Cotopaxi. Reuben probably helped the other children and the women collect the coal from the railroad tracks and pack it back up the mountain to be used in their stoves. Coal, which burns hotter and lasts longer than wood, made it possible for the colonists to keep their stoves burning during the long, freezing nights.

The women of a neighboring German colony also helped. The Germans shared their meat and eggs and offered advice and companionship. Finally, the Jewish people of Denver sent food, cash, shoes, and clothes to replace the colonists' threadbare garments. During the cold winter evenings, Mr. Moshcowitz, one of the colonists, entertained Reuben and the other children with storytelling, magic tricks, and by playing the music box he'd brought with him from Russia.

Warmer weather finally arrived. In April, men walked twenty-six miles to Salida to buy special flour for the Jewish Passover celebration. The colonists hoped for a better year. They planted their crops early, but this time, a late spring blizzard killed the young seedlings. At eight thousand feet, the new plants had little chance of surviving the snow and cold.

In the spring of 1883, many of the colonists departed, and by the end of 1884, the colony was officially dissolved. No one wanted to move back to the overcrowded neighborhoods of New York City, where people squeezed into tiny apartments and trash was left to rot on the streets. Most of the colonists stayed in the West: Colorado, Nebraska, or Wyoming. A few moved as far away as California and South Dakota. Every family received a payment of one hundred dollars to help with moving expenses.

Reuben, his family, and many other colonists moved to Denver. The colonists in Denver built successful businesses, including hardware stores, real estate companies, stockyards, and packaging houses. Many of the Russian Jews served the community as policemen and firefighters, and the colonists helped start many new Orthodox synagogues. They became the heart of the West Colfax Jewish community in Denver.

Young Reuben grew up in Colorado, was married in 1891, and had six children. He moved his growing family to New York City, where he held a variety of jobs: peddler, dockworker, and a conductor on a street trolley. He was a hard worker until his death in 1946, and his many descendants are still thriving.

Only two of the colonists returned to Russia—Sholemm Shradsky and his elderly father, who wanted to be buried next to his wife. Two babies, including Reuben's little brother and a fifteen-month-old child, were buried in the Cotopaxi Cemetery. In recent years, their graves have been set off by a fence, with a historical marker in place to preserve and separate them from the newer graves that surround them on the hillside above town.

People often ask what happened to the land that was promised to the colonists. There are records that show that Reuben's father and others filled out papers that gave them the right to occupy the land where they lived. Under the Homestead Act of 1862, a person had to make improvements on the land for five years in order to claim full ownership. But by then the colonists were gone.

The story of the Russian Jews remains a part of the history of the southern Colorado town of Cotopaxi. In modern times, cars and trucks have replaced the trains that once snaked through the Arkansas River canyon. A sign at a pullout along Highway 50 tells the story of the colonists and the impact they had on a small rural community more than 135 years ago. Although many changes have occurred since 1882, the story of the hardships and eventual success of the colonists is remembered and told over and over again.

Today, if you stand on the abandoned railroad tracks in Cotopaxi and look toward the jagged peaks of the Sangre de Cristo Mountains, you can imagine the cold days and freezing nights the colonists survived. You might also hear echoes of the trains from the distant past. And if you look carefully where the well-worn railroad ties disappear between the steep rock walls of the Arkansas River canyon, you might find bits of coal left from when the railroad workers tossed a little extra from the engines as the trains passed through the small mountain town.

Mary Fields PHOTO COURTESY OF URSULINE ARCHIVES, GREAT FALLS, MONTANA

Stagecoach Mary Fields:
Tough and Tender Woman of the West

Vonn McKee

The wolves may have been following for miles. It's hard to tell in a Montana snowstorm. Although the wagon driver knew the road to the mission school well, swirling snow and a darkening sky obscured the rugged narrow lane. The freight wagon was loaded with supplies and foodstuffs for the nuns, the workers, and the Blackfeet Indian girls who lived at St. Peter's Mission.

Shadows crossed the lane. Wolves! The horses reared and, in seconds, the scene turned chaotic—a violent tangle of harness straps, terrified horses, and the lurching wagon. Heavy barrels and boxes shifted, and the wagon turned on its side, throwing the driver onto the ground. All four horses broke free of the wagon and ran away.

Feeling for the rifle and pistol, always at hand in this rugged country, the driver used the tipped-over wagon for cover. Hungry wolves circled, their dark outlines barely visible in the blinding whiteness. Crouched in the snow, the driver watched—only firing a shot when the beasts came perilously close. And so it went on through the night, hour by agonizing hour.

At dawn, the driver stood. The surviving wolves had vanished. Others lay bloody on the snow. Gripping the wagon with enormous hands, the six-foot, two-hundred-pound driver shoved until the freighter groaned, tilted, and finally turned upright on its wheels.

On that night, the wolves had crossed the wrong path. The wagon driver happened to be one of the hardest-riding, surest-shooting, toughest characters in Montana pioneer history— described by newspapers as "the most picturesque character who ever walked the plank sidewalks" of the town of Cascade.

The large black woman, "Stagecoach Mary" Fields, began gathering the scattered supplies and food barrels—including one that had broken, seeping molasses onto the frozen ground. She loaded everything back on the freighter, then trudged across the snowy field to find her horses.

Mary Fields was born a slave, possibly in Tennessee, but little is known about her early years. After the Civil War, all slaves were granted freedom by the United States government. For the first time in her thirty-three years, she could travel and work wherever she pleased. Mary found work on a paddle wheeler steamboat called the *Robert E. Lee* as a maid, emptying the chamber pots that served as overnight restrooms.

She was lucky enough to be onboard when the *Robert E. Lee* competed in a famous race with rival riverboat the *Natchez* in 1870. The racecourse was the Mississippi River from New Orleans to St. Louis—about twelve hundred miles. The thrilling race between the two riverboats was an international event, and people lined the banks of every town along the route—cheering, shooting fireworks, and placing bets on which boat would reach St. Louis first. There were tense moments: mechanical problems, treacherous sandbars. A thick wall of fog threatened the safety of the steamers.

Years later, Mary Fields loved telling how the crew of the *Robert E. Lee* stoked the wood box with everything from empty barrels to bacon and whole hams just to keep up speed. One writer said that "sparks filled the sky" as the wood-fueled *Robert E. Lee* and the coal-powered *Natchez* battled upriver. In the end, the *Lee* won by more than six and a half hours—and that record still stands.

Eventually, Mary Fields found work as a babysitter and housekeeper for a family in Virginia, whom she may have met during her time on the *Robert E. Lee*. When the family moved to Ohio, Mary followed. With the size and strength to do the work of most men, Mary became a janitor and groundskeeper at a convent, where Catholic nuns lived. Already, her personality reached large, and sometimes troublesome, proportions. She liked her whiskey and cigars and was known for her coarse language and quick temper—not unusual behavior for rough and tough men on the 1800s frontier, but unfitting conduct for a woman—especially a black woman.

An unlikely friendship with one of the nuns, Mother Mary Amadeus, changed Mary's destiny—a turn in her path that would transform the spirited former slave into a larger-than-life Old West celebrity. When Mother Amadeus and five other nuns moved to western Montana to establish a mission and school for Blackfeet Indian girls, she left her friend Mary Fields behind in Ohio.

Cascade, Montana, was beautiful but rugged country, with harsh unpredictable weather. The nuns' temporary living quarters, described as "a crude log cabin," were drafty and poorly furnished. Mother Amadeus, overworked and undernourished, fell ill with pneumonia during the long, brutally cold winter. When Mary heard about this, she traveled to Cascade to take care of her ailing friend. Thankfully, Mother Amadeus recovered. Mary stayed to be near her and would call Montana her home for the rest of her life.

Over the next several years, Mary Fields helped build most of the structures for what became St. Peter's Mission. She wore men's coats and hats—always with a long skirt and apron—and did heavy chores, such as digging holes, hoisting stones to make walls for the school, and taking care of the mules, horses, chickens, and cows. She also drove a freight wagon, sometimes traveling over a hundred miles round trip on rutted dirt roads to deliver supplies back to the mission. Those trips could take several days. Often, Mary picked up visitors at the train depot and gave them rides. One passenger made the entire journey thinking the tall, broad wagon driver wearing an overcoat and cap was a man. Mary was such a brave, reliable driver that she became known as "Stagecoach Mary."

She was notorious among local saloons for her love of strong drink and occasional unruliness. She started many a fistfight and won them all. And Mary never went anywhere without her rifle. Tucked under her apron was a Smith & Wesson .38 caliber revolver, just for added protection.

Stagecoach Mary's habits of wearing men's clothing and getting into occasional brawls at drinking establishments didn't please the bishop who oversaw the area's Catholic missions. Eventually, he insisted that Mary leave St. Peter's. Mother Amadeus couldn't do anything about the bishop's decision, but she arranged for Mary to try out for a job driving a mail wagon.

Several applicants showed up to be the "star route" mail driver—a job contracted by the United States Postal Service—all of them men except for sixty-three-year-old Mary Fields. The job would go to the one who could hitch up a six-horse team to a wagon the fastest. It took a lot of skill to get that many horses into position, put heavy collars on their necks, then fasten the complex harness of bridles, straps, reins, and rings.

Mary, who had years of experience harnessing and driving teams, finished hitching all six horses to the wagon in far less time than anyone expected. The story goes that, not only did Mary easily win the contest, but she had time left over to go have one of her whiskeys and a cigar! And so it was that Stagecoach Mary Fields became the first black woman in history, and only the second woman of all, to deliver the US mail. She faithfully met the train to pick up the bags of letters and, during snowstorms, she would strap on snowshoes, throw the mailbag over her shoulder, and deliver it on foot. Mary drove the mail wagon until she was about seventy years old.

Stagecoach Mary wasn't all toughness and wild ways. After her retirement from delivering mail, she opened a restaurant in the small town of Cascade, but the venture didn't succeed, mostly because she gave away meals to those who couldn't afford to pay. Also, it's rumored that Mary may not have been the best cook.

Then she ran a laundry business from her home but, even then, she couldn't quite stay out of trouble. Once, she was having a drink in the saloon and saw a man walk by who owed her two dollars for a laundry bill. She chased him down an alley and punched him squarely in the face. When she returned to her table, she announced that the man's bill had been paid in full.

Stagecoach Mary had a tender side. She loved children and frequently did babysitting. It's said that she spent most of her wages buying candy for the boys and girls. She loved gardening and spent a lot of her time in her yard tending flowers—pansies being her favorites. Mary was a passionate fan of the local baseball team and would take bouquets of her flowers to give to the players. Now and then, in true Stagecoach Mary fashion, she would shout profane insults to the umpire for making calls against her beloved team.

The whole town of Cascade celebrated Mary's birthday every year—sometimes twice a year if Mary decided to add a celebration! The mayor gave Stagecoach Mary permission to drink in any saloon, overruling a state law that made that illegal for women. The local hotel provided free meals for their cherished former mail carrier.

When in her early eighties, Mary became ill and sensed she didn't have long to live. She wrapped herself in a blanket, walked to a nearby field, and lay down—ready to die. A couple of boys she had once babysat for found Mary, and a friend took her to a hospital in Great Falls, about thirty miles away. Sadly, Stagecoach Mary passed away from liver failure on December 5, 1914. Her body traveled home by train, and her funeral, held in the town's theater, was one of the largest ever in Cascade's history.

Stagecoach Mary Fields, one of the strongest, most fearless women of the West, is buried on a gently sloping hillside overlooking the magnificent Montana landscape she loved so well. It's fitting that the cemetery lies along the same road, between Cascade and the stone ruins of the old St. Peter's Mission, that Mary traveled by wagon countless times—delivering mail, molasses, lumber, friends, and strangers alike—through skin-blistering heat, pounding rain, and bitterly freezing wind and snow.

Many stories about Mary Fields are more legend than fact. For instance, "Mary's friends claimed if a fly lighted on the ear of one of . . . her four [horses] . . . that if she was a mind to she could break the fly's hind leg with her whiplash and then shoot its eye out with her revolver."

Truth, legends, and all—Stagecoach Mary Fields earned her rest on that quiet Montana hillside, and her unique place in Western history.

Solomon D. Butcher, Camera-Toting Pioneer

Nancy Plain

Solomon D. Butcher, twenty-four years old, called himself a "tenderfoot" and boasted that he hadn't done a hard day's work in the past twelve years. Still, when the rest of his family decided to become homesteaders—pioneers—on the Nebraska prairie, Solomon went along.

It was March 1880, and bitter cold. The Butchers left their home in Illinois in two white-topped wagons and began rolling west. Seven weeks and seven hundred bone-rattling miles later, they reached their chosen spot: Custer County, Nebraska. They were now in the middle of the Great Plains, the immense and beautiful region that stretches from the Missouri River to the Rocky Mountains and runs north from Texas all the way into southern Canada.

Resting their horses, the Butchers looked around and saw only one farmhouse, like a tiny island on the land. All the rest was endless sky and grass and gusting wind. The family's wagons—"prairie schooners," they were called—seemed like boats on a sea, a sea made of earth and waves of grass. There wasn't a tree or a bush in sight.

Without timber, the Butchers did what other pioneers were doing—and what some Indian tribes had done for thousands of years on the treeless plains: They became "sodbusters." They built their house out of the root-tangled earth itself, plowing up thick strips of grassy soil and stacking them like bricks to form a roof and walls. "My first experience in sod laying," wrote Solomon, "consisted . . . in wearing out my hands and patience." It didn't help that before they were finished, the Butchers ran out of food and had to eat horse fodder, poisonously flavored with spilled kerosene.

The newcomers then set themselves to planting corn, trudging up and down the field behind a plow, under the broiling prairie sun. Solomon was starting to feel like a fool for leaving his comfortable life back East to "lay Nebraska sod."

The Butchers were part of the flood of settlers who came to the Great Plains after the Civil War. Between 1865 and 1890, more than one million emigrants settled in the state of Nebraska alone. They came because the United States government was giving away land, land that had only

Sylvester Rawding family sod house, north of Sargent, Custer County, Nebraska LIBRARY OF CONGRESS
PRINTS AND PHOTOGRAPHS DIVISION, PHOTOGRAPH BY SOLOMON D. BUTCHER, 1886

recently been the home of the Plains Indians. In 1862, President Abraham Lincoln had signed
the Homestead Act, which provided 160 acres free to anyone with the will to build on a section
and farm it—to "prove it up"—for five years. And there were millions of acres for the claiming.

Homesteaders came from Europe and from all over America. Many arrived with only a
couple of dollars in their pockets. They had never owned much of anything before, let alone 160
acres of land. "Every lick we strike is for ourselves," wrote one thankful young woman. "There are
no renters here."

Yet on the plains, the settlers would face extreme hardships—killer blizzards, raging prairie
fires, grasshopper plagues, deadly droughts, disease, accidents, and more. Half of them would give
up and go home.

Solomon Butcher was born in Illinois in 1856. Now, as he struggled with Nebraska sod, he
daydreamed about his hobby: photography. As a teenager, he had learned how to make tintypes

(an early type of photograph made on a sheet of metal), as well as other techniques of the craft. He was still drawn to the magic of it, the way he could pluck a moment out of time and make it last. So, soon after he arrived in Nebraska, he set up a photo gallery, the first in Custer County. It had dirt floors, a leaky roof, and an old, rat-chewed wagon cover for a photo backdrop. "Such an outfit!" Solomon joked. "It made us sick at heart." Even so, he was able to line up customers. "Whenever anyone wanted a tintype, I dropped my hoe and made it, and went back to the field again."

In 1886, after years of racing back and forth between cornfield and camera, Solomon dreamed up the biggest idea of his life. He called it his "history scheme." He would give up farming altogether and become a traveling photographer, taking pictures of everything he saw on the Nebraska plains. He would collect pioneers' "thrilling stories," too, and put photos and words together in one large book. "From the time I thought of the plan," he wrote, "for seven days and seven nights it drove the sleep from my eyes." When word of his scheme got around, though, settlers on nearby farms shook their heads and told him to return to his crops instead. Behind his back, they called him a "fool" and a "crank." But, said Butcher, "I was too much interested in my work to pay any attention to such people."

He was thirty years old, with a wife, Lillie, and two children, Lynn and Madge, when he borrowed his father's wagon and horses, rigged up a darkroom in the wagon bed, loaded his heavy wooden camera and glass-plate negatives (these were used instead of film in Butcher's time), and took to roaming.

It was June on the prairie. Grasses rippled under the wide blue sky, and the air was sweet with wild roses. There were almost no roads then and no bridges across the streams. At night, coyotes howled under a million stars. Solomon's horses pulled his "picture wagon" over Nebraska's changing terrain—flat tablelands, rolling hills, canyons carved deep by winding waters. The photographer stopped wherever he found a farm or ranch and unloaded his camera. Many of his fellow homesteaders had left behind family members that they might never see again. Maybe Solomon's history scheme wasn't such a bad idea, after all, they began to think. What better way than a photograph to show their new lives to the folks back home?

One of Butcher's first photographs was of his neighbors, the Chrisman sisters—Hattie, Lizzie, Lutie, and Babe. Babe Chrisman, who posed next to her horse, Jessie, told Solomon how she had survived the Schoolchildren's Blizzard of 1888, so named because it happened when the children were at school. Babe was a teacher at the time. She said that the sky had turned almost black at noon. The temperature plunged twenty degrees in no time as a wicked wind and heavy snow tore across the land. Babe let the sure-footed Jessie lead her and her pupils home. But this was a storm so blinding, so fierce, that some people got lost just walking from house to barn and froze to death. Others, stranded on the prairie, never came home. The Schoolchildren's Blizzard was one of the deadliest in Nebraska history.

When the Chrisman family had first come to Custer County, the sisters had cried to see such a "desolate" place. But by the time Solomon pointed his lens, they were successful ranchers, herding cattle on horseback for hours each day. Ranchers had discovered that the grasslands that had once fed millions of buffalo were also "a perfect paradise" for raising cattle. They established enormous ranches, and quite a few got rich.

The cowboys, who worked the range, usually didn't get rich. They were in it for the freedom and adventure. Theirs was a dangerous life too. A young wrangler named J. D. Haskell wrote to Solomon about a stampede caused by a midnight storm. The second the cattle started running, Haskell wrote, he jumped on his horse and galloped at top speed to keep pace with the frightened animals. "The darkness was intense. A terrible wind drove the rain in sheets. The entire herd jumped to their feet . . . and started on a wild stampede before the storm." His horse stumbled once, but the cowboy hung on. "The roar of 4,000 hoofbeats, mingled with the crash of thunder, made it a race never to be forgotten. The cattle could only be seen . . . at the flash of the lightning, which was so dazzling as to almost blind [the] eye." Haskell finally managed to slow the herd and turn it around. But he had come within an inch of being squashed flat into the mud under those four thousand hooves.

Not all the wranglers were men. Butcher photographed cowgirls too. One was a Miss Sadie Austin, who posed for her picture with a rifle in one hand and a pistol tucked into her belt. According to Solomon, Sadie was also "an accomplished musician." Another cowgirl—and ranch owner—was Sarah Finch, an expert at throwing a lariat. Sarah managed her outfit alone for long periods of time, and Butcher knew her well. "A braver [woman] never trod the soil of Nebraska," said he.

Sarah's husband was a pioneer named Ephraim Finch, known fondly to all as "Uncle Swain." He described to Butcher one of the grasshopper invasions that had tormented settlers during the 1870s. First Uncle Swain had seen what looked like a huge cloud. Then he heard "a continuous cracking and snapping sound . . . [that] increased to a perfect roar." Soon "every green thing in sight was . . . hidden with a seething, crawling mass several inches in depth." He could hear their jaws chomping as they devoured all his corn.

Farms were destroyed as the hoppers ate crops and everything else in sight, including leather boots and lace curtains. They even crawled down into the earth to feast on the new potatoes. Uncle Swain reenacted for Butcher's camera how he had tried to smash the hoppers with a tree branch. Since there were no grasshoppers around when Butcher took his picture—the insects had mysteriously disappeared after 1877—the photographer scratched a "swarm" of them onto his glass negative.

Solomon never took himself too seriously and liked to have fun with his work. He would often use a sharp tool to carve images, such as those hoppers, onto his negatives. He would draw on the negatives, too, with ink, wherever he saw the need. A bunny here, a tree there, a flock of ducks on the wing.

At least once, Solomon's sense of humor got him out of a jam. One day, he accidentally poked a hole in a negative. To cover up the spot, he painted over it an enormous turkey, which showed up white in the finished print. Years later, Butcher recalled what had happened when he brought the picture to Theodore Hohman, the farmer who had ordered it:

"Mr. Hohman said, 'What is that?' The photographer trembling in his shoes remarked, 'Looks like a turkey.' Hohman said it couldn't be as the turkeys were not around. Besides they did not have any white ones. His wife spoke and said, 'Yes Theodore don't you remember me telling you to drive the turkeys away.' That settled it. But to this day I expect Hohman wonders where that old white gobbler came from." Solomon named this photo "The Power of Suggestion."

He posed most of his subjects in front of their soddies. With walls three feet thick, these dwellings were cool in summer, warm in winter. But it was impossible to keep the outdoors from coming in. Wrote one woman, "Life is too short to be spent under a sod roof." After a heavy rain, it was drip, drip, drip from the ceilings, followed by gobs of mud. Mice, rats, fleas, and bedbugs— "enough to stampede a flock of cowboys," wrote one man—liked to nestle in the walls. Snakes did too. All these critters wriggled inside from time to time to pay a visit, sometimes even dropping from the ceiling into a pot boiling on the stove. A boy went to wake his sister one morning, only to find a rattlesnake curled by her head on the pillow. He stood frozen in horror until the snake finally slithered away through a hole in the wall.

Solomon loved to photograph children. He pictured his niece Alice milking her favorite cow. He photographed other kids clutching their favorite toys, eating watermelon, perched on horse-back, or harvesting hay. Since the young were needed on the farm, school sessions—in one-room schoolhouses—were short. Books and teachers were scarce too. One teacher was only fourteen years old when she was hired: "If I fail you, you need not pay me," she said.

Although children worked hard, they also enjoyed carefree days when they had the run of the prairie. They went exploring with their dogs and trotted their ponies through saddle-high grass. They hunted for birds' nests, caught tadpoles in the creeks, picked wild plums and wild cherries. Summer brought sparkling sunlight and warm winds. In autumn, the grasses turned red and brown and gold, and the air filled with the scent of fresh-cut hay. One Custer County woman remembered her childhood of long ago: "Those pioneer days, dewy summer mornings, millions of prairie flowers everywhere, frogs croaking, prairie chickens booming and ducks quacking in that, their own country."

In 1886, the same year Butcher began his travels, the first trains chugged into Custer County. With the railroad came a stream of goods and people, and Solomon saw the prairie settling up fast. He was in a hurry now to capture the sod house era—what he called the "Wild West"—before it was replaced by stone and brick and civilization.

Crisscrossing the prairie, taking photographs and collecting stories, Butcher managed to scrape together a living. Then, in the 1890s, came an epic drought. It smothered the land like a thick blanket and by 1894, wrote one farmer, it had "burned everything to a crisp." With their crops shriveled to dust, Nebraskans had no money for photos, so Butcher sold none for most of that decade. There was nothing for him to do but go to work on his father's farm until the long dry spell ended.

In 1899, just as Solomon was recovering from the drought and reviving his photography business, his house caught fire. Everything he owned, including all the pioneers' writings, turned into a smoking heap of ashes. Luckily, his glass plate negatives—all his photographs—survived because they had been stored a short distance away from the house, in the barn. And Butcher had what he called "Western push and energy"; he refused to give up his history scheme. He quickly gathered a new batch of stories and selected the photographs to illustrate them. In 1901, with financial help from his good friend Uncle Swain, Butcher published his book, *S. D. Butcher's Pioneer History of Custer County, and Short Sketches of Early Days in Nebraska*. It had been fifteen years in the making.

Solomon continued to photograph Nebraska until well into the new century, adding to his collection until it included more than three thousand extraordinary photographs. Together they form the most complete record we have of life during the sod house era.

Butcher saw so many changes on the prairie that he was able to make "before and after" images. One sodbuster he photographed had come to the plains with only twelve dollars but was now pictured in front of his grand, gingerbread-carved Victorian mansion. What had once been just clusters of shacks on the prairie had become modern towns, with telephone lines, streetlights, and every kind of store. In the early 1900s, the automobile came to Nebraska, and Solomon was there too, with his camera.

Butcher sold his collection in 1913, for a depressingly low price, to the Nebraska State Historical Society. The history-loving photographer died in 1927, at seventy-one years old, not knowing how grateful the nation would one day be for his priceless legacy. For he had accomplished what he had set out to do: Tell the story in words and pictures of the generation that settled the Great Plains. His photographs show not just the pioneers themselves but their whole way of life—how they worked, what they built, what they loved. Wandering the prairie with his camera, Solomon was a memory keeper. To see his pictures is to turn back the clock to a time that is gone forever.

One Nebraskan told him, "There may be better people somewhere in the world, but I have never met them." Solomon understood the people he photographed because he was one of them. In his pictures, the pioneers' faces show the courage and determination they had needed to survive in their strange new land. Solomon Butcher himself had the same type of grit, even though he held a camera more often than a plow.

Theodore Roosevelt and the River Pirates

Bill Markley

Theodore Roosevelt was fighting mad. Thieves had stolen his rowboat. Standing on the west bank of the Little Missouri River at his Elkhorn Ranch, in what is today western North Dakota, he vowed not "to submit tamely and meekly to the theft." He needed that rowboat to cross the river to check on his horse herd and hunt wild game. He raced to saddle his horse, Manitou, thinking to chase after the desperadoes, but his ranch hands stopped him. It was late March 1886; the river ice had just gone out. The river was swollen. Even if he caught up with the thieves, he would not be able to reach them through the jammed ice floes along the riverbank. His men told him they would build him a boat in three days and chase after the thieves. And that's exactly what they did.

Back in September 1883, the twenty-four-year-old, upper-class New York adventurer Theodore Roosevelt had stepped off the Northern Pacific train in the small town of Little Missouri in the Badlands of Dakota Territory.[1] The bespectacled Eastern dude wanted to shoot a bison before the animals were all killed off. After days of chasing and missing them, Theodore brought down his buffalo. By then he had fallen in love with the West, so before he returned to New York, he bought the Maltese Cross Ranch, south of Medora, and hired men to buy cattle and run the place.

In New York in 1884 Theodore's wife, Alice, and his mother, Mittie, died the very same day—Valentine's Day—and in the very same house. Theodore wrote, "The light has gone out of my life." Alice's nickname for him had been "Teddy." Even though many people called him that, after Alice's death, Theodore did not want to be called by her favorite name for him.

A few months after the deaths, on June 9, 1884, Roosevelt returned to the Badlands to establish a new ranch, where he could grieve in solitude. Rancher Howard Eaton told him to ride along the north-flowing Little Missouri River. Roosevelt would find his solitude thirty-five miles north of the new town of Medora, along the river's west bank, far from any neighbors. He

---

1 The town of Little Missouri faded away and was replaced by the nearby town of Medora.

Little Missouri River runs through Theodore Roosevelt National Park in North Dakota.
GETTY IMAGES / ZACK FRANK / 500PX

happened upon the skulls of two elk, their antlers interlocked in death, so he named his ranch Elkhorn.

Roosevelt employed Maine backwoodsmen Bill Sewall and Sewall's nephew, Wilmot Dow, to build his cabin and manage his ranch. The first step was to cut down trees for the cabin. Roosevelt overheard a ranch hand ask Dow how many trees the men had cut down. "Well, Bill cut down fifty-three, I cut down forty-nine, and the boss, he beavered down seventeen."

Roosevelt brought cattle to the ranch and kept his horse herd on the east side of the river. Most of the year the Little Missouri's flows are low enough so that a person can walk across, but during the spring floods, the only way across is by boat, so Roosevelt had one on hand, tied to a stout tree.

The day he discovered that his boat was missing, did he suspect anyone? Did he know that three desperadoes had decided that the Badlands had become too hot for them? The fact is, local folks suspected them of cattle rustling and horse thieving and would just as soon shoot them or string them up.

Mike Finnigan, known as "Redheaded Mike," was the outlaws' gang leader. The others in the gang were Chris Pfaffenbach, nicknamed "Dutch Chris," and Ed Burnstead, whom Roosevelt would call "the half-breed." One evening shortly before the boat theft, Finnigan became rip-roaring, pass-out drunk in a Medora saloon. Finnigan wore his red hair shoulder length and sprouted a bushy beard. Johnny Goodall, a practical joker, borrowed scissors from the barbershop. Goodall and friends then hoisted the unconscious Finnigan from the floor onto a billiard table, where Goodall cut off all the hair on one side of Redheaded Mike's head and shaved off the beard and mustache on the same side of Mike's face. Goodall even cut the fringe off Finnigan's hunting shirt on that same side. The next morning when Finnigan came to and looked in a mirror, he flew into a rage and stormed into the brush, where he took potshots at townsfolk until Police Chief Arthur T. Packard rode up behind him and knocked him out.

Finnigan and his two shady friends lived in a shack along the Little Missouri, twenty miles upstream from Roosevelt's Elkhorn Ranch. They had an old leaky boat that they shoved off into the water to begin a hasty journey downriver and out of the country. The three desperadoes came upon Roosevelt's boat and decided to take it. They cut the rope that moored it to its cottonwood tree. In the process, one of them lost a mitten. With their new craft, the boat pirates continued north downstream, hoping to reach the Missouri River and disappear.

The next morning, Roosevelt and his men had planned to cross the river to hunt mountain lions. But when Bill Sewall went to the boat to make it ready, he found only the cut rope and dropped mitten. It wasn't easy for Sewall and Dow to persuade Roosevelt to wait while they built a new boat, but finally, he agreed. Realizing that he needed to stay out of their way, he occupied his time reading Tolstoy's nine-hundred-page novel *Anna Karenina*, and writing the first chapter in his biography of Thomas Hart Benton.

It didn't take Roosevelt and his men too much detective work to deduce that the thieves had to be Redheaded Mike Finnigan and his gang. No one else had a boat, and the only way to approach Roosevelt's own boat without being seen would have been by river. And finally, Finnigan and his men and their leaky tub were missing from their shack.

After three days of building, the boat was finished, but frigid temperatures and a blizzard delayed the men's departure.

Roosevelt had a strong sense of justice. It was wrong for someone to take something that did not belong to him. Since there was no law enforcement nearby, Roosevelt, by virtue of being chairman of the Little Missouri River Stockmen's Association, was determined to bring the outlaws to justice.

Few people lived downstream of the Elkhorn Ranch. It was Badlands country, a rugged terrain of twisting ravines, jagged buttes, and crumbling mud and sandstone cliffs.

Six days after discovering the theft, Roosevelt, Sewall, and Dow finally set off on their adventure. Once committed to the river, there was no turning back. The swift current, with ice floes jammed along the shorelines and steep banks of crumbling slippery mud and sand, made it difficult to climb onto the shore. And there were no downstream neighbors with whom they could spend the night, no shelter from the elements. Roosevelt wrote about his men, "They were tough, hardy, resolute fellows, quick as cats, strong as bears, and able to travel like bull moose."

Roosevelt's posse was miserably cold. It was tough trying to stay dry and keep the sand and mud out of everything. Roosevelt sat in the middle of the boat, while Dow paddled in front and kept a lookout for ice floes and logs, and Sewall steered from the rear.

The wind was a problem. At one moment, it would blow from behind, helping to speed them along. At other times, it would swing around and blast them from the front, or suddenly switch from one side of the river to the other. Sewall grumbled, "It is the crookedest wind in Dakota."

Roosevelt's posse had provisions for two weeks, but they still looked for game along the way. They shot prairie fowl and two deer to supplement their food supply.

Three days after the posse began its chase, the men spied Roosevelt's stolen boat, along with another tied to the bank. Smoke rose from a fire off in the sagebrush. Roosevelt and his men quietly moored their boat and crept toward the camp. A man sat near the fire tending it, his weapon on the ground near him. Roosevelt and his men got the drop on him. It was Dutch Chris, and he offered no resistance. He told them that the others were out hunting.

Roosevelt, Sewall, and Dow settled in to wait for their arrival. Here is what Roosevelt later wrote about what happened next:

The camp was under a lee of a cut bank, behind which we crouched, and, after waiting one hour or over, the men we were after came in. We heard them a long way off and made ready, watching them for some minutes as they walked toward us, their rifles on their shoulders and the sunlight glinting on their steel barrels. When they were within twenty yards or so we straightened up from behind the bank, covering them with our cocked rifles, while I shouted to them to hold up their hands—an order that in such a case, in the West, a man is not apt to disregard if he thinks the giver is in earnest. The half-breed obeyed at once, his knees trembling as if they had been made of whalebone. Finnigan hesitated for a second, his eyes fairly wolfish; then, as I walked up within a few paces, covering the center of his chest so as to avoid overshooting, and repeating the command, he saw he had no show, and, with an oath, let his rifle drop and held his hands up beside his head.

Now what to do with the prisoners? Roosevelt was concerned that they might try to escape. The temperature dropped below freezing every night, so if the prisoners' hands and feet were bound, they might become frostbit. Roosevelt decided to make the outlaws take off their boots. That way they would not attempt to run off through the cold and the prickly cacti. The campfire was well stoked against the frigid night as Roosevelt, Sewall, and Dow took turns guarding the prisoners.

Roosevelt planned to float down the Little Missouri to the Missouri River and then make his way by river two hundred miles to Mandan, where the posse would hand the thieves over to the authorities. The next morning, all the men got into the boats and paddled downstream. In the following days, they battled ice floes, making only a mile or two a day. Then they came upon a massive ice jam that blocked their way downriver. As they waited for the ice jam to break, Roosevelt finished Tolstoy's tome. He asked the thieves if they had any reading material. Finnigan gave Roosevelt his dime-novel life of Jesse James, which Roosevelt promptly devoured. To make matters worse, the party, having doubled in number, was rapidly consuming its food supply. Close to being completely out of food, the men resorted to making unleavened bread, with flour mixed with muddy river water.

Roosevelt gave up trying to reach Mandan and decided to march the thieves fifty miles south to Dickinson. Sewall hiked out of the river valley to search for a ranch but found none. The next day, Roosevelt and Dow did the same on the opposite side of the river and found a cow camp. The camp's lone cowboy fed Dow and Roosevelt and gave them more food for the others. The cowboy told them that there was a ranch fifteen miles to the east, where they might be able to get supplies and find transportation.

The next day, Roosevelt borrowed a "wiry bronco" from the cowboy and rode to the Diamond C Ranch near the Killdeer Mountains. The rancher there agreed to sell Roosevelt supplies and hired out to him a team of horses and a wagon, with himself as driver. Meanwhile, Sewall and Dow were marching the prisoners toward the Diamond C Ranch. When Roosevelt and the rancher met up with them, the rancher shook Redheaded Mike's hand, saying, "Finnigan, you damned thief, what have you been doing now?"

Sewall and Dow returned to the boats to wait for the ice jam to break so they could head downriver to Mandan, where they would be able to transport their boats by rail back to Medora.

Roosevelt, with the driver and the three prisoners—Redheaded Mike, Dutch Chris, and Ed Burnstead—left for Dickinson. Roosevelt did not trust the rancher after discovering that he and Finnigan knew each other. Neither did he feel safe riding in the wagon, for fear Finnigan and friends would try to overpower him. Instead Roosevelt trudged behind, with his Winchester resting on his shoulder. As he hiked along, the sun began to thaw the ground, turning it into deep gumbo mud. It made for a hard slog. Finally, the men came to a homesteader's cabin, the owner of which allowed them to spend the night. Roosevelt made the three desperadoes sleep in a top bunk, while he sat on the floor with his back to the door. With his Winchester cradled in his arms, he stayed awake all night. Next day, the party continued its journey to Dickinson, where Roosevelt handed his prisoners over to the sheriff.

Roosevelt's next concern was to take care of his feet. He asked the first person he met on the street the whereabouts of the doctor's office. The man he had asked just happened to be Doctor Victor Hugo Stickney himself. Dr. Stickney took Roosevelt to his office to care for his raw, blistered feet. Stickney wrote, "You could see he was thrilled by the adventures he had been through." Roosevelt told Stickney he was "pleased as punch" to have had an adventure. Then, after cleaning off two weeks of Little Missouri mud, Roosevelt hopped on the next westbound train to Medora to attend the spring meeting of the Little Missouri River Stockmen's Association.

The thieves were tried in Mandan in August 1886. Roosevelt dropped the charges against Dutch Chris, stating that he was "not capable of doing either much good or much harm." Finnigan and Burnstead were sentenced to twenty-five months hard labor in the Dakota Penitentiary in Bismarck.

But that's not the end of the story. In 1887, Finnigan wrote a letter to Roosevelt, explaining why he and his friends had stolen the boat. Finnigan said that he and Burnstead were sorry for what they had done, and that Burnstead was in poor mental health. He also asked if Roosevelt would intercede for them so that they could leave the penitentiary early. At the end of his letter, Finnigan wrote, "P.S. Should you stop over in Bismarck this fall on your Western tour, make a call to the Prison, I should be glad to meet you."

Did Roosevelt have compassion for the thieves? We don't know, but Finnigan and Burnstead were released from prison five months early.

Many people living in the Badlands in Roosevelt's time thought that he should have taken justice into his own hands and hanged the outlaws from the nearest cottonwood tree. As Roosevelt would later write, "In any wild country where the power of the law is little felt," men tend to believe in taking immediate revenge on the wrongdoers. But he wanted the thieves tried in court because he had a strong belief in the rule of law. And he lived by this belief. It gave him a moral foundation and would guide him when he became president.

Years later, Roosevelt wrote to Senator Albert B. Fall, "Do you know what chapter . . . in all my life . . . looking back over all of it . . . I would choose to remember; were the alternative forced upon me to recall one portion of it, and to have erased from my memory all other experiences? I would take the memory of my life on the ranch with its experiences close to nature and among the men who lived nearest her."

John Muir:
Roaming and Writing on the Range of Light

Ginger Wadsworth

"Living is more important than getting a living," John Muir told his father when he was seventeen.

He was tired of working twelve hours a day on the family's farm in Wisconsin to clear fields, build fences, or hoe long rows of wheat. His seven brothers and sisters were exhausted too. Their father granted them two vacation days per year, and sometimes a free Sunday afternoon.

The family had emigrated from Dunbar, Scotland, to the United States when John was ten. In Dunbar, his grandfather had been John's first teacher. Grandfather pointed out letters and numbers on shop signs in town, and John quickly learned them.

John was good with his hands and fascinated with how things worked. Under his grandfather's supervision, he whittled and carved little ships and clocks. Other days the pair explored the surrounding countryside, where John first learned to listen to and look at the natural world.

Before leaving for America, John attended primary and grammar school. But when his family settled in Wisconsin, he and his siblings were not allowed to return to school. Their father wanted great wealth to carry on his church's work, even if it meant treating his children like slaves. If he saw them pause from their endless farm chores to take a sip of water, he might flog them for idleness. Upset neighbors grumbled, "Old Man Muir worked his children like cattle."

Unlike his brothers and sisters, John didn't need much sleep. Nights were his free time, and sometimes he walked the dusty roads around the farm by moonlight. "I would spend hours with my head up in the sky. I soared among the planets and my thoughts."

In the dark, he read borrowed books by candlelight. After his father allowed him to have an arithmetic book, John learned algebra, geometry, and trigonometry. He dared not light a fire in the kitchen for warmth during the winter nights. It would anger his father for wasting wood. Instead, wrapped in layers of clothing, he descended into the freezing cellar to construct various gadgets made with discarded bits of wood and metal. He missed his grandfather, far away in

John Muir, 1902 LIBRARY OF CONGRESS PRINTS AND PHOTOGRAPHS DIVISION

Scotland, while he whittled a series of measuring instruments—barometers, hydrometers, and eventually, a clock.

His sisters giggled about another invention—a bed that worked like an alarm clock. John rigged it so that levers and wheels tipped the bed forty-five degrees and tossed the sleeper out of bed. The girls proudly claimed that John was a genius.

Eventually, a neighbor encouraged John to exhibit his bed and his other creations at Wisconsin's agricultural fair. Maybe someone in a machine shop would hire him. John decided to go to the fair, but leaving the farm and his family was a difficult decision. Everyone except his father hugged John goodbye before he boarded the train to nearby Madison, Wisconsin.

His inventions were a huge hit, and John was awarded a special cash prize for his work. After the fair, John rambled over the hills surrounding Madison, swam in nearby Lake Mendota, and made friends.

John wrote to his sisters of reading nature-themed books by Henry David Thoreau and Ralph Waldo Emerson. They inspired him, and for the first time ever, John picked up a journal to record his daily thoughts and discoveries. He would do this for the rest of his life.

He met several college professors affiliated with the University of Wisconsin. They recognized John's unique talents and fine mind, and they encouraged him to attend the college. John signed on as an "Irregular Gent" and moved into a dorm room. To save money he lived on graham crackers and oatmeal. Everyone was curious about the shaggy-headed farm boy in homespun clothes and stopped by to check out his geological and botanical specimens and chat with him.

By the time John was twenty-five, constant talk of slavery and the ongoing Civil War surrounded him and the rest of the country. City living still overwhelmed him. John had never seen dancing, card playing, or even couples kissing! He penned in a notebook that he was "tormented with soul hunger" and abruptly left Madison.

He wandered or worked for a while, always studying new things and places. He and his brother Dan walked to Canada to find work. A few years later, John rambled alone from Wisconsin to the Gulf of Florida, but the humid temperatures in Florida made him ill. After reading an illustrated brochure about the many natural wonders of Yosemite in California, he decided to explore the region.

John Muir was almost thirty years old when his schooner sailed into San Francisco Bay in 1868. Although it was some twenty years since gold had been discovered in California, San Francisco was crowded and noisy. Thousands of miners, fortune seekers, and ordinary citizens still bustled about, scheming about how to strike it rich.

The clamor and frenzied pace weren't for John. He penciled a letter home saying he had arrived in San Francisco, but he was moving on.

He asked for directions to Yosemite.

Several miners pointed southeast and laughed. No pack animals laden with supplies? No guns or knives for protection? Just a bone-thin man in a well-worn traveling suit, wearing a slouch hat and carrying a knapsack.

John took off, carrying a few crusts of bread, his tin cup, and some tea.

Once he left San Francisco and its thick coastal fog, it was as though his mind also cleared. He paused on a ridgeline to peer east. And there they were—the Sierra Nevada—sharply outlined against the blue sky.

The jagged, snow-capped mountain peaks took his breath away. He longed to explore this famous range and its "glorious ranks and groups, [with] snowy robes smooth and bright." Yosemite Valley was nestled among these peaks.

He crossed California's wide, fertile Central Valley on foot. The valley gave way to oak-covered foothills that led to steeper mountains. By now John had walked hundreds of miles. He felt healthy and happy and frequently belted out familiar Scottish songs he'd learned as a boy.

At last he reached an overlook where, way below him, a waterfall edged an emerald green valley. Wind blew the water sideways, and John at first believed it was a "dainty little fall . . . only about fifteen or twenty feet high." Was this in the famed Yosemite Valley he had longed to see? He couldn't wait to find out!

John zigzagged downhill, as sure-footed as any mule. He pushed through brush, forded creeks, and easily bounded from boulder to boulder. Finally, the rock-rimmed Yosemite Valley (seven miles long and one and a half miles wide) stretched before him. He gasped. It was more spectacular than he'd imagined.

The Merced River meandered through meadows mixed with black oaks and pines. Rock walls, some thousands of feet high, cradled the valley. A monolith stood sentinel-like at the far end. It was Half Dome.

When John finally reached the base of his "dainty little fall," he looked up and laughed. Bridalveil Fall dropped hundreds of feet (actually 620 feet). Water bounced off boulders bigger than houses.

Wind whistled through the pines in Yosemite Valley; a symphony of birdsong surrounded him. Other thundering waterfalls crashed over cliffs, and grasses grew everywhere, mixed with flowers. Yosemite resembled a lush garden, giving John a powerful sense of peace.

After a few days, he was out of money and food. He walked back to the Central Valley to harvest crops, run a river ferry, and break horses for people he had met on his initial trek from San Francisco. Every day he dreamed about Yosemite: "The mountains are calling me and I must go."

He was back in Yosemite Valley the following spring. It was perfect timing. The continental railroad officially linked the East with the West on May 10, 1869. Now many Easterners could more easily explore the West, and that included Yosemite.

Accommodations in Yosemite were simple, so John went to work for James Hutchings, a valley hotelkeeper, helping him build a sawmill to cut pines and oaks into the lumber necessary to house these new tourists.

John built himself a one-room cabin that straddled a creek. He called it his "hang-nest." He hung up a hammock and made shelves. Some held borrowed books; others overflowed with his growing collection of cones, rocks, feathers, plants, and more. From his hammock, John peered through a skylight that framed a bit of Yosemite Falls, while below him the creek would "sing and warble in low sweet tones."

When he had time off, John's idea of an easy weekend hike was to cover fifty miles. Few people could keep up with the wiry Scotsman. He might bed down on a mattress of fir boughs or a boulder in the middle of a creek. And he climbed peak after peak and grew to love the mountains even more. "It seemed to me the Sierra should be called . . . the Range of Light," he penned.

He often explored the nearby Mariposa Grove of Big Trees, where six hundred giant sequoia trees grew. Their size and beauty overwhelmed John. He estimated that it would take about twenty people holding hands to circle the trunks of some of the ancient ones. As always, he stuffed his pockets with treasures and filled his flower press with specimens. He wrote, "When we try to pick out anything in nature, we find it hitched to everything else in the universe."

Waterfalls fascinated him, too, especially Yosemite Falls, North America's highest waterfall. It plummeted some 2,400 feet to the valley floor. One day, while John was scaling the talus, or rock-strewn slopes beside the fall, he spotted a ledge nearby—behind Lower Fall. Without considering the danger, he inched sideways along the slime-covered ledge until he could look directly "down into the heart" of the falling water. Water surrounded him; spray drenched him. This death-defying experience, when adventure overcame his sense of reason, was something John would experience many times.

He liked to sit on North Dome, overlooking the upper end of the Yosemite Valley, to think about how the valley, with its steep granite walls, might have been formed. He knew that Josiah Whitney, California's leading geologist at the time, believed that some major event had caused the land to sink, exposing the granite domes and walls and creating the valley. John was not sure he accepted that theory.

On his forays into the surrounding canyons and valleys, he dropped to his hands and knees and examined rocks and boulders cut by glacial ice. Some were a different color and composition than others, meaning, John believed, that they had come from elsewhere. Glaciers were large, slow-moving sheets of ice that push rocks and debris to gradually gouge the earth underneath, and he was beginning to suspect that they had carved out Yosemite Valley.

To test his theory, John set out lines and stakes to measure any movement of ice in the backcountry's remaining glaciers. He kept careful notes and drew illustrations. After learning more from his observations and measurements, he spoke up.

"I can show you where the mighty cavity (the Yosemite Valley) had been grooved and wrought out for millions of years. . . . I can take you . . . to see for yourself how the glaciers have labored, and cut and carved."

Josiah Whitney considered John an "ignoramus," dismissing the self-taught geologist's statement. But John was earning a solid reputation as an expert on Yosemite. He guided visitors around the valley and shared his knowledge. They sought him out for advice, often asking him for the best hiking trails to take, and scientists corresponded with him about his various theories.

Professor Joseph Le Conte, a geology professor from the University of California at Berkeley, journeyed to Yosemite to talk to John about glaciers. The two spent several days on horseback, exploring the mountains surrounding Yosemite Valley.

Step by step, John explained how and where he had done the research leading to his conclusions on glacier formation. His systematic, detailed approach, in addition to the fact that he recorded all his observations in notebooks, convinced experts like Le Conte that John was right.

John's long, nature-oriented letters were also popular. Friends told him he was a natural storyteller, that he made faraway places come alive. With encouragement, he gave up his mill work to write. His first nature essay, "Yosemite Glaciers," was published in the *New York Tribune* on December 5, 1871. John earned two hundred dollars for his "pen work," a lot of money at that time. Just maybe, he could survive financially on his writing.

He eventually authored hundreds of articles for national magazines. As his fame as a naturalist grew, he also published natural history and travel books, much like his early heroes Ralph Waldo Emerson and Henry David Thoreau.

John's influence in Yosemite and the natural world drew many to visit him, including Ralph Waldo Emerson and several American presidents. President Theodore Roosevelt camped with John in Yosemite for three nights in 1903, a trip that resulted in Roosevelt's protecting 148 million acres of forest and wilderness land from development. Thanks to Roosevelt, Yosemite Valley and the Mariposa Grove of Big Trees became part of Yosemite National Park.

John often said that one of the happiest days in his life was May 28, 1892. That's when he and his friends started the Sierra Club, an organization that today remains one of the most popular environmental groups in the Western world.

In his later years, John traveled extensively, including to South America and to Alaska, still filling his little journals with sketches and notes about geology, flora, and fauna. But Yosemite Valley was always on his mind, and he couldn't stay away for long. It was "the grandest of all the special temples of Nature I was ever permitted to enter."

A Boy, Bloomers, and Baseball in the West:
Smoky Joe Wood and the Bloomer Girls

Johnny D. Boggs

Joe Wood would not have called himself a professional baseball player during the late summer of 1906, although he got paid for playing.

Two and a half bucks if Ness City lost. Five dollars for a victory. Back then, when the average household income in the United States was under nine hundred dollars *a year*, playing baseball for a Kansas town ball team could earn a sixteen-year-old a nice chunk of change. Sometimes, however, just getting to the game proved tiring. When Ness City played Beeler, Joe would ride his bicycle sixteen windy miles west, pitch the game, and bike all the way home. But Joe got to do what he loved: play baseball.

The sport, which started on America's East Coast in the early 1800s, witnessed a surge in popularity across the country after the Civil War (1861–1865). In 1869, the first professional baseball team, the Cincinnati Red Stockings, went undefeated. The professional National League was founded in 1876, and the American League was formed in 1901. Out West, baseball games could be found at army forts, even on American Indian reservations, and in most towns—as long as there were enough players to field a team.

Born in Kansas City, Missouri, in 1889, Joe had moved around a lot with his family: to Chicago, Pennsylvania, Colorado, and Ness City, Kansas. As an old man in the 1960s, he said he had lived through much of the "Wild West" he was now watching being recreated on television: outlaws, posses, and cattle thieves. In the Colorado boomtown of Ouray, Joe had often watched stagecoaches coming from the mines, with armed men guarding gold shipments. The town could get "wild and woolly," Joe remembered, when the miners got paid. When he started playing baseball in Colorado and Kansas, he learned that things could get wild at ballgames too. In those days, towns took baseball seriously. Amateur teams didn't just play for fun. Civic pride was at stake.

STAR BLOOMER GIRLS BASE BALL CLUB

627 W. MICHIGAN ST. INDIANAPOLIS, IND.

Postcard showing ten members of the Star Bloomer Girls Base Ball Club, wearing baseball uniforms emblazoned with a star LIBRARY OF CONGRESS PRINTS AND PHOTOGRAPHS DIVISION, CHICAGO: CROSS PRINTING CO., [CA. 1905]

"The ball game between two rival towns was a big event back then, with parades before the game and everything," Joe explained years later. "The smaller the town the more important their ball club was. Boy, if you beat a bigger town they'd practically hand you the key to the city. And if you lost a game by making an error in the ninth inning or something like that—well, the best thing to do was just pack your [suitcase] and hit the road, 'cause they'd never let you forget it."

In August 1906, "the kid wonder of the base-ball world," as one Kansas newspaper called Joe, got the chance of a lifetime: Play baseball for a nationally known team that grabbed headlines and packed baseball fields across the West. Joe would be paid twenty-one dollars a week to finish the season—roughly nineteen games. Plus, he wouldn't have to bike his way to town after town; he would be riding with the players on a special train to Ellinwood, Hays City, Great Bend, and even Wichita. But there was a catch. He would be playing usually as "Lucy Totton," not Joe Wood.

That's right. Joe Wood started his professional career playing on what was supposedly an all-girls team.

It started after Ness City's town team played host to the Kansas City Bloomer Girls on Monday, August 27. Joe played shortstop for the boys, who won 23–3, before more than five hundred spectators, "the largest crowd gathered in this city for a number of years to witness the National game," the *Ness County Times* reported. How big was that crowd? Well, Ness City's population was barely five hundred in 1900 and just more than seven hundred in 1910, according to US Census records.

Bloomer Girls baseball teams formed across the country in the 1890s and rose in popularity in the early 1900s. They took their name from Adelaide Jenks Bloomer (1818–1894), an activist for women's rights who also created the then-popular baggy women's underdrawers that were also called bloomers. Although Vassar and other colleges had female baseball teams, many people thought women had no business playing any kind of athletics—including bicycling or even just walking for exercise. Back in those days, women could vote only in Wyoming, Colorado, Utah, and Idaho, and wouldn't be granted voting rights across the nation until 1920. Equal rights, you see, were a long way off.

In 1906, therefore, a team of girls playing a team of boys might be considered naughty—and sure to draw a crowd. Bloomer teams would take 75 percent of the profits for each game, but the remaining money was usually enough to satisfy the all-male local amateur and semi-pro teams.

"This was now serious baseball," historian Gai Ingham Berlage wrote, and some teams "used a little creative dishonesty to make sure their teams were competitive." One of those dishonest teams was the Kansas City Bloomer Girls (sometimes called the Boston Bloomer Girls, or the National Bloomer Girls, or just the Bloomer Girls). Using male players disguised as women, owner/manager Logan Galbreath figured, would make his team more competitive. That's why, after the Ness City game, Galbreath asked Joe if he would be interested in playing for the Bloomer Girls.

The rest of the conversation, Joe recalled to historian Lawrence S. Ritter, went like this:

"Are you kidding?" I asked. I thought the guy must have been off his rocker.

"Listen," he said, "you know as well as I do that all those Bloomer Girls aren't really girls. That third baseman's name is Bill Compton, not Dolly Madison. And that pitcher, Lady Waddell, sure isn't Rube's sister. [George Edward "Rube" Waddell (1876–1914) was a star pitcher for the American League's Philadelphia Athletics at the time.] If anything, he's his brother!"

"Well, I figured as much," I said. "But those guys are wearing wigs. If you think I'm going to put on a wig, you're crazy."

"No need to," he says. "With your baby face you won't need one anyway."

"Joe has a girlish face," *The Hutchinson News* reported, "and it was easy for him to pass as a girl." After getting permission from his father, Joe became a "topper," the name given to men disguised as women (for the wigs most of them wore).

On Saturday, September 1, the *Ness County News* reported: "Joe Wood went with the Bloomer Girls to play ball with them for about two weeks." Some players, parents, and newspapers would not identify a boy playing on an allegedly all-girls team. As the *Emporia Gazette* humorously reported: "An Emporia boy, whose name is withheld because it is his first [offense] and also on account of his parents, is playing baseball in another state with the Boston Bloomer girls."

Joe and his teammates journeyed from town to town in style. "They travel in a private palace car," a newspaper reported. The Bloomer Girls also brought a fourteen-foot-high canvas fence that could turn pastures into ballparks—and prevent cheapskates from watching the games without paying the admission, usually twenty-five cents for adults, ten cents for children. The team also had its own grandstand, capable of seating two thousand, that was equipped with a canopy to protect spectators from the sun.

Men always played the pitcher and catcher positions for the Bloomer Girls, said Joe, who also played shortstop. He and his three male teammates would put on their uniforms in the hotel—"we didn't have clubhouses or locker rooms in those days," Joe said—before going to the ballpark. Most of those attending the games, Joe said, likely realized not all the players were girls, but sometimes the spectators were upset to learn of the impostors. A headline in *The Leavenworth Post* proclaimed: "Some of the Girls Shave Regularly and Chew Tobacco, in Fact They Aren't Girls."

Before Joe joined the team, a woman realized that some Bloomer Girls were men when they boarded a streetcar with her after a game in Fort Scott. "No woman," she told a reporter, "ever had a face like that."

"They are not the handsomest women that ever ate Boston baked beans," a Baxter Springs, Kansas, newspaper reported, "but are stout healthy, agreeable and astute girls, who take a good natured roast, and give back as good as is sent." Another newspaper described the Bloomer Girls as "five tough women and as many nondescripts."

Yet the Bloomer Girls didn't just rely on Joe and other men to play competitive ball. One of Joe's teammates, Kansas City's Ruth Egan (1892–1958), had signed with the Bloomer Girls a year earlier, when she was just twelve years old. With her mother traveling with the team as her chaperone, Ruth often played first base with a catcher's mitt and later traveled with other mixed-sex and women's barnstorming teams into the 1920s. Years later, Ruth held the world record for the longest throw of a baseball by a woman: 253 feet, 4.5 inches. Ruth even caught a baseball dropped five hundred feet from an airplane.

It's difficult to document exactly where Joe played baseball with the Bloomer Girls during that summer of 1906. Newspaper accounts are not always reliable, and owner Galbreath reportedly had two Bloomer Girl teams crisscrossing Kansas at the time. Sometimes, Bloomer teams were playing on the same day in different, and distant, Kansas towns.

Most of the scores were close, Joe recalled, although he said the Bloomer Girls won only eight games. One newspaper cited its team's loss to the Bloomer Girls because, "Our boys were too chivalrous to beat the girls."

On Monday, September 16, Joe returned home, the day after the Bloomers lost, 4–3, to Wichita. But Joe's abilities had gotten him plenty of attention. A short time later, he joined the Cedar Rapids (Iowa) Rabbits, of the independent Illinois-Indiana-Iowa League. The next year, the Rabbits sent Joe to the Hutchinson (Kansas) White Sox, of the Western Association, where the speed of Joe's pitches earned him a spot on the American Association's Kansas City (Missouri) Blues. By 1908, eighteen-year-old Joe was pitching for the major league's Boston Red Sox.

In 1912, Joe—now known across the nation as Smoky Joe Wood because of how hard he could throw—pitched the Red Sox to the World Series title, earning three victories against the New York Giants in the championship series. Overall, Joe spent fourteen years in the major leagues, primarily as a pitcher, then an outfielder, with Boston and the Cleveland Indians. He posted a 117–57 record as a pitcher and batted .283 in his big league career. In 1922, Joe became head baseball coach at Yale University, where he coached for twenty seasons and became the first major leaguer to be given an honorary degree from Yale. Joe, who died in 1985 at age ninety-five, was never elected into the Baseball Hall of Fame, but one Hall of Famer, legendary pitcher Walter Johnson (1887–1946), said, "There's no man alive that could throw harder than Smoky Joe Wood."

Bloomer Girls baseball teams gave "hundreds of women the opportunity to earn a living playing baseball," historian Debra A. Shattuck wrote. But Galbreath's team also gave a young Kansas boy his first big break.

Joe Wood, however, wasn't the only future big league baseball player to play for a girls' team. In 1912, while Joe was pitching the Red Sox to the World Series, Galbreath hired a teenager named Rogers Hornsby (1896–1963) to play for the Bloomer Girls in Dallas, Texas. Hornsby later spent twenty-three seasons in the big leagues, leading the St. Louis Cardinals to the 1926 World Series title and was inducted into the Baseball Hall of Fame in 1942.

"So," Joe said, "I'm not in such bad company."

Earl Bascom and His Bronc-Bustin' Brothers: Fathers of Modern Rodeo

Rod Miller

One day in 1995, a rancher in Saskatchewan, Canada, was tidying up in a storeroom. A box about the size of his billfold tucked away on a cluttered shelf caught his eye. He blew off the dust and lifted the lid. Inside was a shiny trophy belt buckle—the kind awarded to rodeo champions. Engraved on the buckle were the words *Earl Bascom, All-Around Champion Cowboy, 1930 Three-Bar Ranch Rodeo*. The rancher likely wondered: Who was Earl Bascom?

Earl Bascom loved horses. He said one time, "The horse is my life and specialty." And, like many cowboys, he especially liked horses that bucked. Or, in cowboy lingo, horses with a bellyful of bedsprings, horses that pitch, duck and dive, come apart, or bust in two. The kind of horses they call gut twisters, high rollers, cloud hunters, or sunfishers.

Riding out the storm on a bucking horse is a young man's game, but Earl started earlier than most. He had ridden horses before he could walk, and by age three could ride alone. But one day, while riding through a meadow with his father and brothers, the horse Earl rode was stung by a bee. The horse didn't like that and started jumping and kicking in fright. Earl hung on to the bucking horse for all he was worth and rode out the storm, staying in the saddle until an older brother rode up beside him and plucked him from the back of the pitching horse.

Earl's first bucking horse ride happened on the family's 101 Ranch in eastern Utah's Uintah Basin, not far from a community called Naples and a town named Vernal. His grandfather, Joel Bascom, started the 101 Ranch after coming west across the plains with the Mormon pioneers. John Bascom, Earl's father, was a young man when the family settled in the Uintah Basin. He worked as a cowboy on ranches around the area. He also wore a badge, serving as a Uintah County deputy sheriff and as constable for the town of Naples, and rode with posses chasing the famous bandit Butch Cassidy and his Wild Bunch and other outlaws.

Earl Bascom riding a Brahma bull in 1939 COURTESY OF JOHN BASCOM

John married Rachel Lybbert, a girl from a neighboring ranch, and started a family of "Bronc-Bustin' Bascom Boys." Raymond, called Tommy, was born in 1901, Melvin "High Pockets" in 1903, Earl in 1906, and Weldon "Preacher" in 1912.

The growing boys got around on four legs more often than two, going horseback after cattle, breaking and training horses, and often riding to school and church. With their father's help, they put on little rodeos of their own, climbing aboard calves, colts, donkeys, and even sheep. Hanging on to manes, wool, leather belts, and loose ropes wrapped around the animals' bellies, the boys learned the balance and fast reactions required to stay aboard buckers of all kinds—and, when bucked off, they plowed furrows in the dirt with their noses, raised clouds of dust when landing like a bag of dirty laundry, spit out grit from between their teeth (swallowing more than a little mud in the process), and covered themselves with bumps and bruises. But, most of all, they had barrels of fun becoming the Bronc-Bustin' Bascom Boys, instilling in themselves the belief that they could ride anything with four legs and hair.

But life on the 101 Ranch was not always a good time, for when Earl was but six years old, death came calling. Cancer took his mother, leaving Earl's father to raise the family on his own. Feeling a need for a change from the dry, overgrazed, and increasingly barren Uintah Basin, John Bascom packed the children and all they could carry into a covered wagon and headed southwest toward Price, Utah. A week or so later they reached the railroad there and boarded a train bound for Canada.

The paint was barely dry on the new town of Raymond, Alberta, when the Bascoms arrived. Raymond was settled by, and named for, Ray Knight, whose wealth came from Utah mines owned by his father, Jesse. Knight invested in miles and miles of Canadian prairie grassland, raising cattle, horses, and sheep by thousands. John Bascom worked as foreman for Knight, and the boys worked as well.

Despite all the livestock to be tended, not all the work was horseback. Earl said, "I remember when the prairie began to be fenced. Ray Knight put in a fence 100 miles long. My brothers and I and others dug post holes and set cedar posts for miles—100 posts per man per day was the standard."

Still, there was plenty of cowboy work to do. Earl remembered taking part in a big horse roundup. The cowboys swept the prairies from places called Writing-on-Stone, Sweetgrass Hills, Manyberries, and Purple Springs, gathering some seven thousand horses. Earl said the horse herd, in places a mile wide, was the prettiest sight he had ever seen.

All those horses in Earl's life further spurred his interest in rodeo, and it was in Canada where the Bascom boys' bronc-riding careers began in earnest. But there was also schooling to consider.

As was the case at most out-of-the-way places at the time, formal education for Earl was often erratic. Rural children were often kept out of school for days, even weeks and months at a time to help out with work, or for other reasons. When Earl was in third grade, schools closed to help stem the spread of a flu epidemic. When the teacher shooed him out the door and closed it behind him, he thought his school days were at an end. He could read, after all, and wasn't that good enough?

But the next year a Mountie—an officer in the Royal Canadian Mounted Police—came by the ranch to see why Earl was not in school and insisted he return. Getting sent back to the classroom took a strange turn this time around. Earl's father arranged to provide school bus service of a sort to students in the area. He fitted out an old stagecoach and hitched up a team of horses to pull it and assigned Earl to drive the route, picking up his classmates in the morning and taking them home in the afternoon.

Earl turned out to be a good student, advancing through his studies quickly and succeeding in athletics. He showed a talent for art and took lessons by mail, including instruction developed by renowned Western artists Charles M. Russell and Frederic Remington, both distant cousins of the Bascoms.

None of this, however, interfered with his love for horses and rodeo. He and his brothers broke and trained horses as part of their ranch work. They also helped put on rodeos, as well as ride in them, at ranches and in communities around the area. While working at one ranch, Earl and Weldon helped try out more than one thousand horses to select the best buckers for rodeos. The ranch owner liked to watch the Bascom boys try his broncs. "The higher they threw us the wider he grinned," Earl said.

From about the age of twelve on, Earl was a fixture in rodeo arenas all over Canada, winning more than his share of prize money and trophies. The older he got, the farther he and his brothers traveled, climbing aboard bucking horses across the continent, excelling in the sport for more than twenty years. Earl and some other cowboys spent a few years as church missionaries in Mississippi and put on rodeos to raise money to build a chapel. People there didn't know what to make of the young men from the West in their big hats and tall boots. "Folks had quite a time deciding whether they were called cow-boots or horse-shoes," Earl said.

According to Earl, "a farmer came to the rodeo arena with a mule that . . . would kick, bite, and buck and was mean as a hornet. We decided to use it in a special event at the evening rodeo." They called the event the "Ladies Wild Mule Ride." The saddled mule was led into the arena, and the announcer called for a lady volunteer from the audience to climb aboard. All was quiet at first. Then a young woman in a long dress and sunbonnet left the crowd and sashayed into the arena and swung onto the mad mule.

The mule bucked and pitched and reared and spun around the arena, but the lady stayed in the saddle and rode it to a standstill, to the delight of the audience. No one knew who the lady was, and her identity was the subject of conversation for years afterward.

The truth is the "lady" was really Earl Bascom in a borrowed dress.

"We had a lot of fun putting on those rodeos in Mississippi," Earl said. But as much fun as rodeo was, it was also a business. During the Depression years, it was the only way Earl and others could earn a living at times. Earl won many championships and set many records in the rodeo arena. He also worked as a rodeo clown and bullfighter. But as successful as he was as a competitor, it was as an inventor that Earl earned lasting fame in rodeo.

While in Canada, the Bascom boys developed a new kind of chute for bucking out horses. Rather than roping and "snubbing" horses in the arena so the rider could saddle and mount them (which was often a rodeo in itself), or releasing the horse straight out of the front end of a narrow chute (which sometimes resulted in smashed legs, turning the rider's kneecaps into pocket change), the Bascoms came up with the "side delivery" chute. A wide gate, hinged at the end of the chute near the horse's head, opened at the tail end, forcing the animal to turn out and into the arena from the side.

Earl designed the "muley" saddle-bronc saddle, removing the horn for safety. He came up with the one-handed bareback rigging. He modified chaps, standard equipment for cowboys on the range, to make them more suitable for rodeo riding. Earl and his brothers were the first to host a night rodeo, using electric lights to illuminate the arena. They were the first to introduce Brahma bulls as bucking stock, making bull riding a regular rodeo event.

All these inventions and developments became standards in the rodeo arena, familiar to this day to audiences and contestants everywhere rodeos are held. Their inventiveness earned Earl and the Bascom brothers the titles of "Fathers of Modern Rodeo," and "Fathers of Brahma Bull Riding." They resulted in Earl's inclusion in numerous rodeo and athletic halls of fame across the United States and Canada, along with other recognition and remembrance.

Through it all, Earl kept up his interest and study in art. Those studies got a boost when a horse rolled over on him. "I thought every bone in my body was broken," he said. While recovering, he was encouraged to give college a try, and he enrolled at Brigham Young University in Provo, Utah, to study art. "College wasn't easy for me, I didn't even graduate from high school," he said. "There I was, a 27-year-old freshman and I hadn't been to school in years. I felt like a wild horse in a pen. My mind was as unruly and tough as a horsehide."

He spent seven long years earning a degree, his studies interrupted by rodeo. Earl said, "In order to finance my tuition, board and room, and art supplies, I rodeoed all summer between school years. . . . You had to be good to win and you had to win to keep going." And keep going he did, both in the rodeo arena and at college. And, mirroring his success in rodeo, Earl earned widespread recognition as an artist and sculptor, with works of art housed in several museums as well as private collections. The Professional Rodeo Cowboys Art Association declared Earl Bascom the first professional rodeo cowboy to become an artist and sculptor. He has been named the most famous cowboy artist Canada has produced. And his acclaim stretches across the sea, as the first cowboy ever named a fellow of the Royal Society of Arts in London, England—an organization first founded in the eighteenth century.

There is more, much more, to be told about Earl Bascom and his bronc-bustin' brothers. Earl's story did not end with his death in 1995 at age eighty-nine at his ranch in Victorville, California. He will be remembered wherever horses buck and cowboys climb onto the hurricane deck of those pitching horses to test their skill.

Who was Earl Bascom? The cowboy who won the All-Around Championship at the 1930 Three-Bar Ranch Rodeo had pocketed his cash winnings and was long gone down the road to another rodeo before receiving the trophy belt buckle. The rancher who put on the rodeo had no forwarding address, and in those days it wasn't easy to track people down. So, the buckle went on the shelf. And there it sat until 1995. With the help of modern methods, Earl Bascom was located on his ranch in Victorville, California. Shortly before his death, Earl finally got the All-Around Champion Cowboy trophy buckle he had won sixty-five years earlier.

Unbreakable Navajos

Joseph Bruchac

Two decades ago I was in Washington, DC, to attend the Festival of American Folklife. It's a yearly event that draws thousands of visitors to the National Mall to experience living traditions from around the world. I was there as a Native American storyteller. Among those invited to share their heritage were two friends of mine, Navajo men who had used their native language to play a unique role during the Second World War. On one evening, I went to a reception for festival participants at the Jefferson Library. As I stood there listening to the Marine Corps band, one of my friends, Samuel Smith, wearing his distinctive red cap labeled "Navajo Code Talker," came running up to me.

"Have you seen my buddy?" he asked, scanning the crowd as he spoke.

Out of the corner of my eye I could see that buddy he was trying to find. Keith Wilson, the other Navajo code talker invited to the event, was crouching behind a large, distinguished African American man in a tuxedo. His finger held up to his lips, Mr. Wilson was signaling for me not to give his location away.

I had a hard time not laughing. Keith Wilson, a former Marine PFC [private first class], then in his late seventies, was hiding behind none other than Secretary of State Colin Powell. Keith, along with hundreds of other Navajo volunteers, had used his Native American language of Dineh to send coded messages throughout the Pacific region during World War II. Because our enemies never suspected that United States forces would use Native American languages, these Dineh codes were unbreakable. Now, in the midst of this formal shindig, those two true American heroes were playing hide-and-seek, like a couple of mischievous kids.

I should have expected it. Over the course of the years before and after the publication of my historical novel *Code Talker*, I'd spent a lot of time in the company of numerous Navajo men who'd not just served with distinction, but who had never told anyone outside a small military circle about the unbreakable code they'd created. Until it was declassified in 1968, even their closest friends and their own families knew nothing about it. What impressed me the most about

Corporal Henry Bake, Jr. (left) and Private First Class George Kirk, Navajo Indians serving in a Marine signal unit, operating a radio behind the front lines, Papua New Guinea, December 1943 PHOTO BY USMC/INTERIM ARCHIVES/GETTY IMAGES

every code talker I met, or whose story I had learned, had always been the same things—their courage, their dedication, their modest lack of self-importance, and their sense of humor.

Once I was on a panel at Arizona State University, talking about the code talkers' contribution to winning the war against the empire of Japan. I was sitting next to Samuel Tom Holiday. Sam had enlisted at the age of nineteen and was then in his late eighties. He told the audience a story I'd heard before, about crouching in a foxhole next to another Marine during a night attack. A shell landed near them and the other man started yelling, "I'm hit, I'm hit!" But when Sam turned on a flashlight, what he saw was a huge frog that had jumped in and landed on the other man's helmet. It was a funny story, but what made it even more memorable for me was that every time Sam Holiday said, "I'm hit," he punched my shoulder, an impish smile on his face with each solid blow.

After the panel was over, one of the women in the audience came up to me. "I can see that the code talkers like you," she said. "But why were they beating you?"

Most of the books about World War II, even those written after 1968, make no mention of the role played by the five hundred or more Navajo men who were called upon to send the most crucial radio messages using their native languages. Nor do they mention the other Native Americans—Comanches, Hopis, Mesquakies, and others—who did the same.

Nor do most Americans know how amazing it was that those men, who were fluent both in their own tongues and in English, were still able even to use their indigenous languages. All of them had learned English while at the government boarding schools that had pulled in Native American boys and girls during the last decades of the nineteenth century. But these schools had also enforced the policy of strictly forbidding any language *other* than English. Speaking a single word in Navajo resulted in immediate, harsh punishment.

I'll never forget the story I heard a Navajo man named Carl Gorman tell during an interview in 1996 at the National Museum of the American Indian in New York City. While a young child in a Navajo boarding school, he had made the mistake of greeting one of his white teachers with a polite "good morning" in Dineh: *Yaa-aa-eey*. His teacher grabbed him and dragged him into a basement, where he was chained to a radiator and given nothing but bread and water for several days.

What some might find even more amazing about the way so many Navajo boarding school survivors served so effectively and honorably as Marines is the recent history of the people. The entire Navajo Nation, less than a century before World War II, had been conquered in 1862 by the United States military. The people were then sent on what became known as the "Long Walk" to the Bosque Redondo, a windswept, arid concentration camp in New Mexico. Everyone, from children to elderly men and women, was forced to walk three hundred miles. Hundreds of Navajos died. However, the Navajo people survived as a nation. A few years later, they were allowed to return to their homeland of Dinetah. By 1942, it's estimated that their tribal nation numbered more than fifty thousand.

On December 7, 1941, an event occurred that changed the world. The empire of Japan, which was then trying to gain control of the entire Pacific Ocean, staged a surprise attack on Pearl Harbor in Hawaii. Most of the American fleet was destroyed in the attack, and over 2,400 Americans died. This led to the beginning of America's involvement in World War II. Because of Pearl Harbor, the United States declared war on Japan and its military allies, Germany and Italy.

Despite their own bitter history with the United States, when word of that Japanese attack on Pearl Harbor reached the Navajos, the first thing many Navajo men did was to offer themselves as soldiers. America was, as they referred to it in the code they would create, "Namaha," our mother. Although most of those first Navajos who tried to join the army were turned away because they could not speak English, it was different for those Navajo men who were bilingual. Because they spoke both Navajo and English fluently, the Marine Corps realized that there was a special way they might be used.

The idea of using a Native American language to send radio messages was not a new thing. During the First World War, Cherokee, Choctaw, and other indigenous American soldiers were assigned to send messages in their own tongues. These the Germans could not understand. During the Second World War, the Navajo language was chosen by the Marine Corps for two reasons. First of all, unlike Cherokee and other languages used a quarter-century before, Navajo was not then a written language. Highly tonal and far different from European languages, only Navajos could speak it fluently. Second, thanks to the boarding schools, by 1942 there were hundreds, if not thousands, of Navajo men who were fluent in English (and who had stubbornly retained their knowledge of Dineh).

In that year, a group of twenty-nine such Navajo men was recruited by the Marine Corps. None of them were told their mission until they were taken to a room at a military base in California and ordered to create a secret code using their native language for combat communications. They exceeded all expectations, creating a double, or two-tier, code. They came up with over two hundred terms, such as referring to a submarine using the Dineh word for "fish," or calling a bomb an "egg," and—displaying that Navajo sense of humor—the country of Spain by the words for "sheep pain." And they also included words for the letters of the English alphabet so that things could be spelled out in Navajo. The letter "A" was *wo-la-chee*, the Navajo word for ant, "B" was *shush*, the word for bear, and so on.

Those twenty-nine men became Platoon 382. Not only were they the first all-Indian platoon in Marine Corps history, but they graduated with the highest marks in every area of training. They were proud *Washindon Akalh B-kosi-lai*—United States Marines.

In August of 1942, with the invasion of Guadalcanal, the Navajo volunteers began to prove themselves as a deadly secret weapon. Navajo code allowed their commanders to coordinate the most complex operations without having the Japanese, who had broken every American code before this, understand a single word. More and more Navajos were recruited and trained.

Many of the new Navajo Marines were in their teens when they enlisted. Some were under the legal enlistment age of eighteen or, if parents gave their consent, seventeen. Because most Navajos back then did not keep birth records, they did not have any legal documents to prove their ages. Families would remember what season someone was born in, but not the day. In some cases families only knew the year of their child's birth. A great many Navajo men were physically smaller than the average Marine. Such men, even if they were in their twenties, might look so youthful that they might be turned away. As a result, Navajo men wishing to enlist would often bring their parents with them to vouch for their eligibility, even if they were not yet seventeen.

One example is a fifteen-year-old Navajo boy who came with his parents to enlist. When asked how old he was, he turned to his parents, who said to the Marine officer, "He is old enough to enlist." And so, he was accepted.

In addition to being smaller on average than other Americans, Navajo code talkers faced another problem because of their appearance. Because their facial features looked somewhat Asian, they were often mistaken for enemy spies. On a number of occasions, Navajo code talkers were arrested or even physically assaulted by other American servicemen who thought they were Japanese soldiers wearing American uniforms.

Samuel Holiday told me that on at least two occasions, men from his unit who knew him had to rescue him from other American Marines who were sure that they'd caught an enemy infiltrator.

One code talker had an even narrower escape. A sailor with a bayonet on his rifle started chasing him, trying to stab him, sure he was going to kill a spy. Luckily, because the Navajo Marine was so small, his clothing was baggy. The bayonet pierced his shirt three times but missed his body while he kept dodging and shouting things like, "I'm an American. An American. New York Yankees. Brooklyn Dodgers!" Finally, other Marines who knew who he was grabbed the attacking sailor and took away his rifle.

Finally, to keep them safe from other Americans, every code talker was assigned a special Marine guard to protect him.

Every major operation in the Pacific relied on Navajo code talkers, and they were credited with saving thousands of American lives. Not only did they use their language to send messages, but they were communications specialists as well. They knew how to operate every kind of wire or radio equipment and often had to set up the electronic communications wires themselves, carrying cable and heavy radios on their backs in the face of enemy fire. From 1942 to 1945 the code talkers were a central part of every United States Marine operation in the Pacific, sending important messages by radio and telephone. When the Marines captured the strategic island of Iwo Jima, Navajo code was used to notify the Pacific command. Word of the atomic bombs dropped on Hiroshima and Nagasaki, as well as the surrender of Japan, were also sent by Navajo code.

The Navajo code talkers returned home when the war ended, but none of them were allowed to mention their special service. They could only say that they were ordinary Marines, not the best trained and strategic of specialists. As Chester Nez, one of the original twenty-nine, explained in an interview in 2004:

When we got out, discharged, they told us this thing that you guys did is going to be a secret. When you get home you don't talk about what you did; don't tell your people, your parents, family, don't tell them what your job was. This is going to be a secret; don't talk about it. Just tell them you were in the service, defending your country and stuff like that. But, the code, never, never, don't mention; don't talk about it. Don't let people ask you, try to get that out of you what you guys did. And that was our secret for about 25, 26 years. Until August 16th, 1968. That's when it was declassified; then it was open. I told my sister, my aunt, all my families what I really did.

Despite the secret they kept, they were honored by their people for their service. Many became teachers, community leaders, and—like Carl Gorman—artists. After 1968, when their contribution was finally made public (since computers could finally send coded messages as fast as could two Navajos), the Navajo Code Talkers Association was formed. Its mission was to tell their stories and to provide educational and cultural support to Navajo youth. At a White House ceremony in 2001, all of the surviving original twenty-nine code talkers were awarded the Congressional Gold Medal.

Today, all of those men I met and every other Navajo code talker have, as we sometimes put it, walked on. Yet their legacy remains, as does the unbroken Navajo Nation.

Fire and Tragedy:
Joe Thurston and the Granite Mountain Hotshots

Rachelle "Rocky" Gibbons

CRASH! A bolt of lightning lit up the sky and ignited a hilltop near the small town of Yarnell, Arizona, on June 28, 2013, starting a chain of events never before seen in history.

Two days after the fire first sparked, an elite group of twenty firefighters called "Hotshots" were called into duty. They headed up the mountain for what they figured would be a routine day of "battling the beast" called fire, and in humble terms, just doing their jobs. Little did they know that only one of their band would survive nature's horrendous attack against them.

One of those valiant firefighters who gave his life that day was my cousin, Joe Thurston, a family man with a loving wife, two young sons, and truly Western roots. I want to tell you about Joe, and about his brothers, known as the Granite Mountain Hotshots.

Joe B. Arthur Quinn Thurston (an initial and two middle names—how cool is that?) was born early in 1981 in Cedar City, Utah. Joe's mother, Gayemarie Ekker, was descended from two pioneer ranching families, the Biddlecomes and Ekkers, and spent part of her growing-up years on the family-owned historic Robbers Roost Ranch in southeastern Utah. Gayemarie's brother and Joe's uncle, cowboy A. C. Ekker, guided Robert Redford through the Robbers Roost area in 1975 on a trek sponsored by *National Geographic*, after which A. C. was featured on the magazine's cover. A. C. tragically died in 2000 from injuries sustained in a plane crash. With cowboying in his genes, Joe Thurston very easily could have followed in A. C.'s footsteps, but he had other aspirations for his life.

Joe was a typical kid who loved skateboarding (he had the scars to prove it), skiing, and playing soccer. In the fifth grade, he received the Hope of America Award from the local Kiwanis Club, and he was a member of the Order of the Arrow in the Boy Scouts of America. When he was twelve his dad bought him a set of drums, and so began a musical hobby Joe would enjoy his whole life. On the other hand, because he played in several rock bands, his neighbors didn't enjoy

Granite Mountain Hotshots crew cutting fire line in the Prescott National Forest, Arizona PHOTO BY TARA ROSS, SUMMIT FIRE DEPARTMENT, CREDIT US FOREST SERVICE GILA NATIONAL FOREST. "WHITEWATER BALDY FIRE 2012" BY GILA NATIONAL FOREST PHOTOGRAPHY IS LICENSED UNDER CC BY-SA 2.0

that hobby nearly as much! Joe grew up and graduated from Southern Utah University, with cum laude honors and degrees in chemistry and zoology.

Joe married his high school sweetheart, Marsena, in 2002. The two remained in Utah for a few years, until Marsena was offered a management position in Prescott, Arizona, and the couple decided to relocate. In Prescott, Joe got a job at a local brewery (that's a place that makes beer) since, harkening back to his chemistry degree, he had aspirations of becoming a brewmaster. He did very well at the brewery but caught the firefighting "bug" when he spent a summer season as a volunteer firefighter with the Groom Creek Fire District. Joe took aim at becoming a Hotshot, training hard and running fourteen miles a day. The day he got the job with the Granite Mountain Hotshots was one of his proudest.

The men and women who become wildland firefighters train for unbelievably long hours in order to be in top physical shape for the job. They are required to hike many miles into fire locations while carrying heavy packs and tools of the trade, such as shovels, rakes called "monkey paws," chain saws, and Pulaskis. A Pulaski is a tool that combines an axe and an adze in one head. (An adze is similar to both an axe and a hoe, with an arched blade at right angles to the handle, and is used to loosen the dirt and rip out brush.)

The most fundamental purpose of a Hotshot crew is to starve a fire of the vegetation that's feeding it by physically removing the grass, shrubs, and trees from the fire's path. The crew establishes and creates a "fire line," which is devoid of vegetation and forms a clear break, sometimes as wide as a road. This, the firefighters hope, will stop a fire in its tracks. It's brutal work. The crews are divided into diggers, sawyers, and swampers. The diggers initially break and scrape the ground down to mineral soil, the sawyers expertly wield the chain saws to cut larger brush and trees out of the way, and their assistants, known as swampers, haul away the branches and brush cut by the sawyers in order to clear the corridor.

Joe's job on the crew was as a swamper for his firefighting partner, Scott Norris. The two made a great team and were good friends off the job as well. All the guys on the crew, even though they had their arguments now and then, were devoted to each other and always "had each other's backs," no matter what. They worked hard, and they played hard, sometimes socializing together at barbecues, or hiking and mountain biking, just for the fun of it.

On June 28, the day the fire started on Yarnell Hill, the Granite Mountain Hotshots were battling a different fire, the West Spruce Fire, in the Prescott National Forest. They wrapped up that fire by eleven that night, and the next day they were called for duty on the Mount Josh Fire, also in the Prescott National Forest. At this time, thirty-seven fires were burning in the state of Arizona, products of the monsoon season and the lightning created by those thunderstorms.

Saturday night, June 29, Granite Mountain's superintendent Eric Marsh received orders for his crew to report to Yarnell on Sunday morning. When the men arrived at 6:30 a.m., the size of the fire was estimated at six hundred acres. That morning the National Weather Service had forecasted a normal monsoon day—an unstable atmosphere with a warm, dry layer of air near the surface. Scattered thunderstorms were predicted, with a risk of strong winds near any that formed. Eric Marsh was assigned to oversee crews working the rear of the fire, or its heel. This was the least active of its borders but was a crucial point of defense. His second-in-command, Jesse Steed, would be responsible for guiding the Granite Mountain Hotshots on the ground.

Before hiking into the wild, the Hotshots attended a briefing at the Yarnell Fire Station, where they received word that the Boulder Springs Ranch had been established as their "bombproof" safety zone, the place they should go if danger was imminent. The boys headed out to do their jobs, trudging along a path on the mountain about 5,400 feet in elevation above the town of Yarnell, along the southern edge of the blaze as the fire marched northward. Their first task was to build an anchor point on the mountaintop—a launching pad or start—for their new fire line. From this point, they could implement their plan of attack. This was accomplished by noon, when the men took a break to eat lunch and watch the fire burning below them. By then the blaze had consumed almost two thousand acres and was moving northeast and away from them, at a half mile per hour. Things were definitely picking up.

After lunch, Granite Mountain Hotshot Brendan McDonough was selected to be the lookout and was transported by a member of another Hotshot crew to a spot about a mile to the northeast. From there he could keep eyes on the fire from a different angle and relay to his crew below him atmospheric and weather conditions as they came in on his radio.

Around 2:00 p.m., pre-evacuation orders were issued for the town of Yarnell, with residents given only four hours to leave. The National Weather Service issued a weather alert. A meteorologist in Flagstaff had spotted on radar a gathering storm that was moving toward the fire's east side, with potential downdraft winds of thirty-plus miles per hour. Winds like these could wreak havoc and turn the already stubborn Yarnell Hill Fire into an absolute monster.

The Granite Mountain Hotshots continued to work diligently cutting a fire line until shortly after 3:00 p.m., when they gathered by a field of boulders on top of a ridge southwest of Yarnell and watched from a safe distance as the fire continued to burn and grow in size. They had received no clear direction from the commanders down below, so they watched and waited, while deciding what to do next.

At 3:30 p.m., a second warning came in from the National Weather Service. It was bad news, confirming that a thunderstorm was indeed approaching from the north on a direct collision course with the fire. The downdraft winds might be fierce, spraying down on the flames at forty or fifty miles an hour. If that storm had contained moisture or rain, it would have helped put out the fire, but unfortunately it only brought high winds.

Up on the ridge with his crew, Eric Marsh was keeping an eye on the approaching storm, after reporting to the command center that the winds were getting squirrelly. His men were presently "in the black," in an area that has already been burned by fire, rendering it a safe place to be, since there was nothing there left to burn. Marsh decided that the Granite Mountain Hotshots should head for the safety zone, the Boulder Springs Ranch, a few miles away. They started picking their way through the black but soon changed to a different route, going directly down into the box canyon leading to the ranch. The canyon was choked with tall, unburned brush that the Hotshots would have to hack their way through, but they seemed confident they could make it to the ranch before the fire got to them. At about this same time, McDonough, the lookout, gauged the fire to be getting too close to his post, so he hiked down and caught a ride out of the burning wild on an ATV, with the same Hotshot who had dropped him off.

Shortly before the men started down the canyon, the impossible happened. The wind direction freakishly shifted by 180 degrees, and a two-mile wall of flames marched southeast, directly toward the unsuspecting Granite Mountain Hotshots. Pushed by vicious winds, the flames doubled in height and sped up to sixteen miles per hour, fourteen hundred feet per minute. Doppler radar measured the height of the smoke plume at 31,500 feet. The crew's view of the fire had been blocked by the thick brush and mountains once they entered the box canyon, and suddenly the inferno loomed from behind a hill to the northeast. A desperate cry boomed on the radio: "Breaking in on Arizona 16, Granite Mountain Hotshots, we are in front of the flaming front!"

The fire rushed at them, and they gave up on reaching the ranch since they couldn't outrun the speeding flames. The Granite Mountain Hotshots had no choice but to immediately clear out a spot around themselves. Sawyers and swampers worked furiously, including Joe Thurston and his partner Scott Norris. After they cleared the area as best as they could in the short time they had, their only option was to deploy their last-resort survival shelters, which are portable cocoons made of layered fiberglass cloth, silica, and aluminum foil. The last communication heard was from Eric Marsh, saying, "Yeah, I'm here with Granite Mountain Hotshots. Our escape route has been cut off. We are preparing a deployment site, and we are burning out around ourselves in the brush and I'll give you a call when we are under the sh- the shelters." The command center immediately responded that they would send the VLAT (vee-lat), which stands for "very large air tanker." The VLAT carried twelve thousand gallons of fire retardant in its belly, but unfortunately time had run out for the brave crew. Try as they might, operations could receive no further answer to their desperate attempts at contact. The Granite Mountain Hotshots had gone silent. It was 4:40 p.m.

The aerial crew circling above confirmed to state dispatchers that survival shelters had been deployed, but they didn't know the exact number, nor the exact location. After the fire had rushed through the area and while the ground was still smoldering, the search by helicopter began. A police officer–paramedic with the Arizona Department of Public Safety named Eric Tarr was aboard, scanning the mountains in search of the shelters. He finally spotted them at 6:19 p.m., at the bottom of a canyon near the Boulder Springs Ranch. Nothing was moving. The chopper landed in a clearing to let Tarr jump out, then flew off to refuel four miles away. Tarr walked uphill, and at 6:35 p.m. he radioed the tragic news: "We have nineteen confirmed fatalities."

In the end, no one ran. The crew stayed together as they always had, and they died together as the band of brothers that they were. The nineteen firefighters who lost their lives while in the line of duty protecting others' homes and property were: Andrew Ashcraft, Robert Caldwell, Travis

Carter, Dustin DeFord, Christopher MacKenzie, Eric Marsh, Grant McKee, Sean Misner, Scott Norris, Wade Parker, John Percin Jr., Anthony Rose, Jesse Steed, Joe Thurston, Travis Turbyfill, William Warneke, Clayton Whitted, Kevin Woyjeck, and Garret Zuppiger. It was the biggest loss of firefighters since 9/11. The only surviving member of the Granite Mountain Hotshots was the one who had served as the lookout, Brendan McDonough.

Were mistakes and bad decisions made? Undoubtedly, but no one person is to blame. The chaotic conditions and circumstances that day combined in the worst possible way, making the Yarnell Hill Fire the "perfect storm" of fires, with tragic results.

After the darkness and black, one must find the light again . . .

After the end, one must find a new beginning . . .

Joe's widow, Marsena, eventually fell in love again and added a little sister, Ember, for her boys to adore and protect.

Joe's mother, Gayemarie Ekker, after facing so much tragedy in her life, remains strong and continues to fight for the Happy Canyon Rim Foundation to protect and preserve historic pioneer and native grounds in southeastern Utah.

In Joe's hometown of Cedar City, Utah, a street has been named in his honor—Joe Thurston Way. It is in a place where he used to fly a kite as a child.

Life does go on, but we must never forget the sacrifice of the Granite Mountain Hotshots.

Holidays on the Frontier

Sherry Monahan

"We're going where?" That's what kids asked when their parents decided to start a new life on the frontier. From the mid-nineteenth to the early twentieth centuries, families loaded their wagons and jostled along unknown lands from Kansas to California. But just because they went west didn't mean that they forgot about holidays. In fact, sometimes the holidays helped families settle into their new lives.

Pioneer families kept many of their holiday traditions regardless of where they lived, whether on a barren prairie or in a city. Decorations, food, and gifts may have been modified from the customs back East, but distance and resources did not stop pioneers from celebrating or keeping up family traditions.

Did people on the frontier observe New Year's? Yes! Ringing out the old year and ringing in the new was a time for celebration on the frontier. New Year's Eve was sometimes observed with balls and parties, but New Year's Day itself was honored much more so than today. From the plains of Nebraska to the big cities across the West, pioneers visited one another's homes on this day. The holiday offered a special chance for friends and neighbors informally to call on each other and give gifts and cards—and also to play games. The card games Hearts, Whist, and Euchre were popular guessing games. Another game, Perception, tested a guest's five senses.

Sometimes pioneers spent the first day of the year touring nearby towns. A young Nebraskan named Ella Oblinger penned a letter to her grandparents, describing her activities on New Year's Day: "January 4, 1883. I take my pen in hand with much pleasure tonight to scratch you a few words . . . New-Years I got a circle-comb, and some candy. New-Years Day I went to St. Peter . . . to see the Asylum but we couldn't get in; their help was all gone but two or three persons but we drove around the building is somewhere between 15 or 20 rods long. Then we all went to the photograph gallery and they all had their pictures taken."

WHY COWS NEED COWBOYS

To Play Perception, or Testing the Five Senses:

For Sight: Arrange items on a tray that is kept out of sight. Bring the items to the participants and allow them to look for one to two minutes. Take the tray away and ask them to write down on a sheet of paper everything they saw. The player who names the most items wins.

For Hearing: Select some musical or other sounds to play. Either blindfold the participants or turn off the lights while each sound is played. The player who correctly identifies the most sounds wins a prize.

For Taste: Select a set number of beverages, fruits, vegetables, or other food items. Blindfold the guests and have them taste the items. The person who gets the most right wins a prize.

For Smell: Select items with a distinct scent, such as a fresh orange, perfume, or vinegar. Have each guest smell the items. The person who gets the most right wins a prize.

For Touch: Select items for your guests to touch, such as cotton balls, grapes, rice, coins, or buttons. Hide them in a paper bag or blindfold your guests. The person who guesses the most right wins a prize.

What was Valentine's Day like? Today most people think of Valentine's Day as a holiday for romantic couples only, but in the 1800s, pioneers held not only private St. Valentine's Day celebrations but public parties and dinners too. To grace walls and windows, hostesses decorated with red and pink cupids and hearts with arrows. Churches, lodges, and hotels, as well as individuals, held St. Valentine's Day festivities. Whether together or apart, pioneers on the Western frontier carried on the traditions of the day in ways not dissimilar to the celebrations of today.

Cards, simply called "valentines," were sent all across America. In 1865, the inhabitants of San Francisco alone received a total of ten thousand. And that number didn't include valentines that were bought from and privately delivered by the city's local card merchants. Most adults sent romantic and sentimental valentines decorated with flowers and lace, while children usually mailed cute or funny ones to friends and family members. Over time, though, adults began to practice this custom too. In the mid-1860s, the *Dallas Weekly Herald* wrote,

The relation that this day had to St. Valentine has long been forgotten. It used to be a practice for gentlemen and ladies to consider the first one they met on this day as their lover or Valentine, and the meeting was usually followed by an interchange of presents. Afterwards it became custom for young folks on that day to interchange anonymous letters, often accompanied with humorous and quizzical pictures. In this country it has come to be a day in which friends of all ages and sexes are at liberty, or take the liberty of interchanging ridiculous pictures—the most so the better—in pretense of ridiculing or burlesquing some peculiar trait of character in the person to whom it is sent. Nothing offensive is ever intended, but rather a presumption of the most intimate relations or cordial friendship; and no one takes offense at anything received, predicated on that day.

How did pioneers celebrate Easter? A lot like today. Easter was a day when children looked forward to colored eggs and hopping bunnies. People dressed in their finest clothes and hats attended church services and enjoyed a special meal. Children colored Easter eggs, but not the way kids do it today. Fresh eggs were wrapped in colored calico or boiled and dyed. Also, imitation eggshells or shells made of candy were filled with confections or jewelry.

Children in Nebraska read a newspaper story about how the custom of celebrating with Easter eggs came about. This was a tale about a pious queen who had sought refuge from her enemies in a remote valley, where her poorest subjects lived. According to the fable, these subjects had never seen a chicken, but they knew about the existence of eggs. One of the queen's faithful servants began delivering to her some chickens, but the people still had not seen them. When Easter came, the queen realized that she had no gifts to offer the children, so she gathered all the eggs her chickens had laid and began to color them. She then hid the eggs around her garden and invited all the children to search for the concealed treasures. As they searched, one child saw a bunny leap from the vicinity of a chicken's nest. The child exclaimed, "Oh, it is a hare that lays the Easter eggs!"

By the early 1900s, candy had become part of the Easter tradition. Marking the holiday with sweets began in a small way in the late 1800s, with a few scattered newspaper ads. But by the turn of the century, advertisements featuring a wide selection of confections filled newspapers across the West. There were cocoa bonbons, cream pecans, crystal nougatines, jelly strawberries, cream filberts, dipped chocolates, Montana caramels, peppermints, marshmallow bananas, and jelly beans—all ready to fill Easter baskets.

Egg dye manufactured by the Paas Dye Company, which is still in business today, was being sold in packets in the 1880s. By 1901, drugstores across the West were selling coloring and decorating kits. A San Diego store advertised "Easter Eggs for everyone . . . the brilliant dyes we sell furnish kaleidoscopic variations of the primary colors. Dyes sold in packets at five cents each, every shade you can think of." These packets were later converted into tablets of dye.

What did Fourth of July celebrations on the frontier look like? The Fourth was often kicked off with a parade or a cannon blast, to be followed by a benediction by the local minister or priest. Speeches by city officials and local business owners were also common, and the reading of the Declaration of Independence was a featured highlight. Most businesses closed on the nation's birthday. People decorated with red, white, and blue and proudly displayed Old Glory. Festivities included races, swimming competitions, band concerts, and the baseball games that have been popular for over 150 years in America. Picnics filled the day, and ice cream was a favorite treat. As in our time, Fourth of July evenings culminated with fireworks, many types similar to those used today. These included rockets, Roman candles, pigeons, squibs, tourbillions, and wheels. Pioneers also sent patriotic postcards to their loved ones when they couldn't be with them.

Miss Nettie Spencer, who grew up in Oregon in the late 1870s, proved how special an event the Fourth of July celebration was in her town by the amount of pies her mother made: "The big event of the year was the Fourth of July. Everyone in the countryside got together on that day for the only time in the year. Everyone would load their wagons with all the food they could haul and come to town early in the morning. On our first big Fourth at Corvallis mother made two hundred gooseberry pies. You can see what an event it was."

After the parades, speeches, and picnics, pioneers enjoyed horse races, pedestrian races, boat races, shooting competitions, and baseball games. Baseball was a big event for many Fourth of July celebrations. Most teams were local or semi-pro until 1876, when the National League was formed. After that, professional games became more common on the Fourth.

Did the pioneers eat turkey on Thanksgiving? That really depended upon where they lived. Thanksgiving was celebrated all over the frontier with many traditional eighteenth-century New England dishes appearing on tables in restaurants and homes alike. Many Western settlers ate turkey, goose, cranberry sauce, pumpkins, pies, and all the trimmings similar to those enjoyed today. Regional items were also featured on frontier tables. These included elk, squirrel, or opossum in Missouri, prairie chickens on the Great Plains, and buffalo tongue in Montana. Regardless of the types of food they ate, frontier families got together on Thanksgiving for a few days of feasting, games, and fun. It was a holiday in which settlers gave thanks to God for the fall harvest and other blessings.

It's true that pie and turkey are synonymous with the celebration, but so is football. Yes, even back in the nineteenth century pioneers played football on Thanksgiving. Early American football was a cross between rugby and the football Americans know today. But no one officiated at these games. The teams consisted of eleven players each and included a quarterback, rushers, halfbacks, and fullbacks. In 1885, some three hundred residents of Kansas City, Missouri, enjoyed a Thanksgiving Day football game. The *Kansas City Times* reported, "About 300 half-frozen spectators assembled at the baseball grounds to witness the match game of football between Monges and Gruber elevens. As an exhibition of skill, the game was not a brilliant one, but as a mirth-producing spectacle it was a howling success. It would be difficult to state by just what rules the match was governed, but as near as could be determined they were a combination of Marquis of Queensbury, go as you please and catch as can catch."

One odd and forgotten Thanksgiving tradition was observed all over the country in the late nineteenth and early twentieth centuries—masquerade balls and parades. These were staged in towns in Washington, California, Iowa, Missouri, and other western and midwestern states, as well as those on the East Coast. It was common for children and adults to wear masks, as they do on Halloween today. In 1902 the *Greene Recorder* in Iowa ran a story called "False Faces." It began, "Thanksgiving time is the busiest season for the manufacturers of and dealers in masks and false faces. The fantastical costume parades and the old custom of masking and dressing for amusement on Thanksgiving Day keep up from year to year in many parts of the country, so that the quantity of false faces sold at this season is enormous. Masks of prominent men and the foremost political leaders are made by some manufacturers, and large-sized false hands, noses, ears, etc. are also new and amusing."

Believe it or not, associating Thanksgiving with shopping is not a new thing. Stores and merchants took the opportunity to offer a variety of holiday-related merchandise for sale and advertised their wares in local newspapers across the West. (Newspapers across the West also printed Christmas advertisements.)

Was Christmas a big deal on the frontier? Yes, no matter where they were, most pioneers recognized the day. Ranchers, businessmen, miners, and almost everyone else could take a break, within reason, from their duties. In isolated settlements, people marked the day with a simple meal, some prayers, and singing. In larger towns across the frontier, Westerners gathered for church services, celebrated with friends, decorated community trees, and more. Throughout the region, church and God were always the focus.

Christmas Eve was generally the day for Santa Claus to hand out presents. Some churches invited orphans and poor children to receive gifts—sometimes as simple as a preserved orange peel to scent a drawer, or a piece of candy. At church, kids also heard choirs sing and helped decorate Christmas trees. (Many people did not have Christmas trees in their homes, while churches and other community gathering places often did. Trees in homes became more popular as the turn of the nineteenth century neared.)

Christmas day itself was usually spent at church and with family. After services, pioneers enjoyed a day filled with feasting, drinking, and merrymaking. Watermelon for Christmas? Yes, in Texas!

Elizabeth Le Breton Gunn, who was living in Sonora, California, penned this letter to her parents on December 26, 1851.

Flathead Indians' pre-Christmas gatherings in present-day Glacier National
Park, Montana LIBRARY OF CONGRESS PRINTS AND PHOTOGRAPHS DIVISION,
BAIN COLLECTION

Yesterday was Christmas Day. . . . We filled the stockings on Christmas Eve. . . . The children filled theirs. They put in wafers, pens, toothbrushes, potatoes, and gingerbread, and a little medicine. . . . They received cake and candies, nuts and raisins, a few pieces of gold and a little money, and, instead of books, some letters. Their father and I each wrote them letters, and better than all and quite unexpected, they found yours, and were delighted. In my stocking were a toothbrush and a nailbrush (the latter I wanted very much) and some cakes and a letter from Lewis. . . . We had a nice roast of pork, and I made a plum pudding. Mr. Christman gave the children some very nice presents; each of the boys a pearl handled knife with three blades, Sarah a very pretty box, and Lizzie a pair of scissors, and each a paper of macaroons.

FOR MORE INFORMATION

"WHY COWS NEED COWBOYS" BY LARRY BJORNSON

The American West is a very big place, and just about every part of it has working cowboys. But in all the West, the toughest and most dangerous cowboying was done in the Texas brush country, or the Brasada, as the Mexicans called it. A land in which everything grows in an endless, crowded tangle of thorns and sawtooth edges. And through this dry and withered jungle, cowboys rode treacherous half-wild horses at breakneck speed, chasing all-wild longhorn cattle with massive horns and 100 percent bad attitudes. But despite the risks and hardships, the cowboys loved what they did. It was a life in which remarkable skill and quick thinking were pitted against countless hazards and extreme challenges. Every day.

For more about life in the Texas brush country, look for the books of J. Frank Dobie. His books, such as *A Vaquero of the Brush Country*, *The Longhorns*, and *Cow People*, are the best descriptions we have of an almost forgotten place and way of life.

"THE LAST DROP: FROM DEATH TO LIFE AT MADISON BUFFALO JUMP"
BY MATTHEW P. MAYO

In the autumn of the years from 500 BC until approximately AD 1500, when Native Americans began using horses for hunting, nomadic tribes of the High Plains such as the Shoshone, Salish, Pend d'Oreille, Bannock, Crow, and Blackfeet hunted on foot to help sustain their people in the coming year. After locating a herd of grazing bison, warriors stampeded the beasts over a cliff's edge, where the bison tumbled to their deaths. This was an effective, if gruesome, method of procuring meat and the raw materials for so much more, including pemmican, bone tools, vessels, garments, tipi coverings, and other items, for every bit of the slain animals was used by the tribe.

Some locations, such as Madison Buffalo Jump in Three Forks, Montana, remained in use for this fascinating hunting method well into the eighteenth century. To learn more about bison drives, there are lots of interesting websites filled with facts and artistic renderings. But nothing tops a personal visit to one of hundreds of bison jump sites throughout the West (there are 360 such sites in Montana alone!). The Madison Buffalo Jump is a prime example, with in-depth placards explaining the history of the site and the many uses Native tribes had for bison, as well as hiking trails that lead to views of the jump site from above . . . and below!

"EAGLE OF DELIGHT: THE PLAINS INDIAN GIRL IN THE WHITE HOUSE" BY JEAN A. LUKESH

In 1821 Eagle of Delight, a teenage Otoe Indian girl from what is now Nebraska, made an epic journey. She traveled with her husband (an Otoe chief) and with chiefs of several other area tribes to Washington City (Washington, DC) to meet James Monroe, the president of the United States. She was the first and only woman to make that journey with those delegates and their Indian agents. But during the several months of that visit, she proved herself to be a charming and intelligent representative of her people. Before she started back home in 1822, her portrait and several others were painted. In 1962, 140 years after that historic visit, First Lady Jackie Kennedy, the wife of President John F. Kennedy, permanently installed Eagle of Delight's portrait in the White House Library, along with portraits of four of the chiefs, including her husband.

You can read more about Eagle of Delight's life in the book *Eagle of Delight: Portrait of the Plains Indian Girl in the White House* by Jean A. Lukesh. If you ever visit Washington, DC, you might also see Eagle of Delight's portrait and those of her traveling companions at the White House.

"ENRIQUE ESPARZA REMEMBERED THE ALAMO" BY WILLIAM GRONEMAN III

In the early months of 1836, a small group of men took a stand in San Antonio, Texas, then part of Mexico. They defied the Mexican Army of General Antonio Lopez de Santa Anna in the name of freedom and independence for Texas, taking refuge in an old Franciscan mission known as the Alamo. Their fight became one of the most famous in American history. Mexican citizens of San Antonio and American and European immigrants to Texas comprised the garrison of the Alamo, including two famous frontiersmen of the American Southwest, James Bowie and Davy Crockett. Among their number were soldiers not as famous but just as brave as Bowie and Crockett. San Antonio native Gregorio Esparza brought his wife and children into the Alamo for their protection when Santa Anna's army appeared. Gregorio Esparza died, as did all of the Alamo's men, but his family survived. His son Enrique, eight years old at the time of the battle, lived to be an old man. These are his memories of the Alamo, told many years later.

You can read more about Enrique Esparza and his memories in *Eyewitness to the Alamo* by Bill Groneman.

"KATIE JENNINGS AND JOHN JENKINS: YOUNG HEROES FOR TEXAS INDEPENDENCE" BY EASY JACKSON

The Mexican government had been overthrown, a dictator declared, and the constitution thrown out. There were no public schools, no freedom of religion, and no trial by jury. Settlers in Texas, then ruled by Mexico, revolted in anger. Battles took place at the Alamo, and later at a little place called San Jacinto. Two young people, John Holland Jenkins and Katie Jennings, whose stepfather and father, respectively, fought at the Alamo, got caught up in the rebellion and proved that courage and bravery don't always belong just to adults. Thirteen-year-old John was determined to join his hero, General Edward Burleson, in the fight for freedom. After the fall of the Alamo, when word came that the forces of the Mexican General Santa Anna were headed their way and determined to annihilate the Texans, ten-year-old Katie galloped her horse through the area, warning the neighbors so they could escape. *The Blood of Heroes* by James Donovan tells the story of the thirteen-day struggle at the Alamo. More about young John Jenkins's journey can be found in his memoirs *Recollections of Early Texas* edited by John Holmes Jenkins III. One of Katie Jennings's descendants, Linda Sioux Henley, has a website showing a beautiful sculpture she made of Katie's daring horseback ride.

"LOTTA CRABTREE: CHILD STAR OF THE GOLD RUSH" BY CHRIS ENSS

Lotta Crabtree, famous child star of the American West, was born Charlotte Mignon Crabtree in New York City on November 7, 1847. In 1852, she came to California with her parents, locating in Grass Valley, where her mother operated a boardinghouse for miners. Lola Montez, the famous dancer, became interested in Lotta and taught her to sing and dance. Lotta became an overwhelmingly popular actress. For half a century she was on the stage, and when she retired, her wealth was counted in millions, all of which she left to charity.

You can read about Lotta Crabtree in the books *The Triumphs and Trials of Lotta Crabtree* by Raymond Baldwin and David Dempsey, and *With Great Hope: Women of the California Gold Rush* by JoAnn Chartier and Chris Enss.

"BOYS ON THE TRAIL: SURVIVING ON BARK AND BURNT RAWHIDE" BY CANDY MOULTON

In 1856 families left England, traveled by ship to Boston and New York, and then took trains to Iowa City, Iowa. There they started living in tents and put their possessions in small two-wheeled carts that they would push and pull another 1,300 miles to new homes in Utah. They did not have enough money to use wagons and teams of oxen or horses to pull them, which is why they used the handcarts. They were all members of the Church of Jesus Christ of Latter-day Saints and were making the trip because of their religion. The boys in this story were with their families and faced unbelievable hardship. Ten handcart companies traveled across the trail from 1856 to 1860.

Learn more about the handcart companies by reading *The Mormon Handcart Migration: "Tounge nor pen can never tell the story"* by Candy Moulton, or *I Walked to Zion: True Stories of Young Pioneers on the Mormon Trail* by Susan Arrington. To research some of the families and learn more about their stories, visit the Overland Trail Database at https://history.churchofjesus christ.org/overlandtravel/.

You can also visit sites along the Mormon Pioneer Trail, including the Handcart Ranch near Independence Rock in Wyoming (west of Casper, north of Rawlins, south of Lander).

"PONY TRAIL TALES" BY QUACKGRASS SALLY

In April 1860 the Pony Express began, with riders carrying mail by horseback across the plains and mountains of the Western frontier. Over the next 160-plus years, the romance, bravery, and wild, adventurous spirit of those riders have inspired novels, films, poems, songs, and historic reenactments. The actual route was officially designated the Pony Express National Historic Trail in 1992, and dozens of historical sites can be found along this almost two-thousand-mile trail. Travelers from all over the world come annually to experience the vast variety of terrains the trail crosses. Today you can explore the restored Hollenberg Home Station in Kansas, see the XP trail crossing into Fort Bridger in Wyoming, and have a letter sent from the original Pony Express headquarters at the Patee House Museum in St. Joseph, Missouri. Although this endeavor only lasted about eighteen months, the Pony Express became one of America's unique and lasting legacies. Even today, the image of a young rider dashing across untamed territory on a horse, determined to deliver the mail no matter the difficulties, ignites our imaginations and inspires our hearts.

You can discover more information from the National Pony Express Association and get a free map of the trail and the XP stations from the National Historic and Scenic Trails Systems office.

"GRASSHOPPERS FOR SUPPER" BY CANDACE SIMAR

In 1873 a scourge of unimaginable proportions fell upon Central North America. Rocky Mountain locusts invaded the prairie lands from Alberta, Canada, to Dallas, Texas, in an area resembling the shape of a huge teardrop. Crops were destroyed and the settlers hoped that the eggs the locusts had laid would not survive the winter. Instead trillions of hungry hatchlings marched across the landscape, devouring every blade of grass and sprouting field. When the hatchlings were old enough to fly, they carpeted the landscape with trillions more eggs, and the cycle repeated itself. This tragedy caused many settlers to give up altogether and nearly bankrupted the plains states.

To learn more about it, check out *The Banks of Plum Creek* by Laura Ingalls Wilder, and *Harvest of Grief* by Annette Atkins.

"HOWDY, PILGRIM: QUAKERS IN WILD WEST TEXAS" BY S. J. DAHLSTROM

Paris Cox was an early pioneer in West Texas. He was also a member of a unique religious group, the Quakers, or the Religious Society of Friends, which was profoundly pacifist. Paris chose to settle and build a town in a place that had been desolate for thousands of years due to lack of regular rainfall, running water, or trees. Other than those obstacles, American Indians still roamed the plains, and outlaws had very little fear of the law. A man who wouldn't kill or fight seemed a bad bet.

The story of Paris's ironic founding of the town of Estacado on the Staked Plains of Texas is both a puzzle and a tale of heroism. Very little has been written about Paris and his aspirations. But general reading about the grit of the pioneers and the arid Llano Estacado can provide additional information. The religious group he was a part of still exists today, and information about it can be found at quaker.org.

"COAL FOR SUPPER" BY NANCY OSWALD

Reuben was eleven years old when he left Russia and traveled with his family across the Atlantic to the mountains of Colorado. He was part of the Cotopaxi Jewish colony, which planned to farm and own land together. From the beginning, things went wrong. The houses the colony members expected to live in were unfinished, and the ground was rocky and unsuited to farming. Their crops failed, and during the first winter, Reuben and the other colonists nearly starved. They lit bonfires to keep the bears away and were visited by Indians who begged for food. The colony's men worked in a local mine for $1.50 a day and hauled heavy logs for the railroad. The women and children walked four miles to collect coal to fuel their stoves and to keep themselves warm. After two years, the settlers were forced to abandon their dreams. They moved to other parts of Colorado and the West to begin again—this time with success.

For fun, look for Reuben's name on this list of colonists: https://kehilalinks.jewishgen.org/cotopaxi/family-names.html. The list was compiled by Jen Lowe, who was a great help during the writing of "Coal for Supper." Also, you may search the internet for photos and more information on the Cotopaxi Jewish colony.

"STAGECOACH MARY FIELDS: TOUGH AND TENDER WOMAN OF THE WEST" BY VONN MCKEE

Former slave Mary Fields fought her way to wild, rugged Cascade, Montana, in the 1880s to care for a sick friend, Mother Mary Amadeus, a nun establishing a mission and school for Indian children. At six feet tall, wearing men's clothing and smoking cigars, Mary helped build the mission and became the first black woman to drive a US mail wagon. She fearlessly delivered food and passengers across the mountains. "Stagecoach Mary" became a legend in Cascade, where she drank (and fought!) with men in the saloons and was also known for her love of children, growing pansies, and cheering for the local baseball team. Mary was born thirty miles from my home in Tennessee, and I have long been fascinated with her story. On a recent trip to Montana, I placed flowers on her grave, in a quiet hillside cemetery overlooking the same road on which she drove her wagon, between Cascade and St. Peter's Mission.

You can find many colorful articles about Stagecoach Mary in historical newspapers (Newspapers.com), and she is profiled in *Portraits of Women in the American West* edited by Dee Garceau-Hagen, *Notable Black American Women* edited by Jessie Carney Smith, and *African American Women of the Old West* by Tricia Martineau Wagner.

"SOLOMON D. BUTCHER, CAMERA-TOTING PIONEER" BY NANCY PLAIN

If Solomon Butcher had thought more about life on the prairie, with its killer blizzards, raging wildfires, and plentiful rattlesnakes, he might never have become a pioneer. After all, he called himself a "tenderfoot" and boasted that he was allergic to hard work. Still, in 1880, when he was twenty-four years old, he climbed aboard his family's covered wagon and traveled to Nebraska to claim free land under the 1862 Homestead Act. Solomon soon learned that he hated farming, so he turned to his hobby, photography, instead. Packing his big wooden camera in a horse-drawn wagon, he took to roaming the treeless plains, taking pictures of his neighbors and of their little houses made of strips of earth, or sod. These settlers faced many hardships but found joy and freedom in their new lives too. Over the next three decades, Butcher created the best record we have of the people who settled Nebraska and the rest of the beautiful grasslands called the Great Plains. That famous photo of the cow on the roof? That's by Solomon.

For more about Butcher, read *Solomon D. Butcher: Photographing the American Dream* by John Carter, and *Light on the Prairie* by Nancy Plain. To see Butcher's wonderful photographs, visit the Library of Congress Prairie Settlement website. There you'll also find letters written by those determined pioneers, the ones who never gave up.

"THEODORE ROOSEVELT AND THE RIVER PIRATES" BY BILL MARKLEY

As a young man in the mid-1880s, future president of the United States Theodore Roosevelt owned a ranch along the Little Missouri River in Dakota Territory. TR—he didn't like being called "Teddy"—had a boat that he used to cross the river. One night, three thieves stole this boat and headed downriver. TR's two ranch hands built a new boat, and TR and the ranch hands then set off downriver themselves. They surprised and captured the thieves. While TR's men continued on the water, the future president took the captured men across the prairie to the town of Dickinson, where they were sentenced to prison. This is a tale of the stamina and perseverance it took for TR to ensure that justice was done.

You can read more about Roosevelt and his Western adventures in the following books: *The Cowboy President: The American West and the Making of Theodore Roosevelt* by Michael F. Blake, *Theodore Roosevelt in the Badlands* by Roger L. DiSilvestro, *Roosevelt in the Badlands* by Hermann Hagedom, and *The Rise of Theodore Roosevelt* by Edmund Morris. And be sure not to miss TR's own writings in *Ranch Life in the Far West*.

"JOHN MUIR: ROAMING AND WRITING ON THE RANGE OF LIGHT"
BY GINGER WADSWORTH

Growing up on a wheat farm in Wisconsin, young John Muir chafed at the endless days of tedious farm work. He dreamed of going to school and exploring the woods beyond the farm.

The summer of 1860 when he was twenty-two, John decided to leave home. He slung his knapsack over his shoulder and set off on foot to discover the world.

His travels led him to Canada, to Florida, and eventually to San Francisco, California. From there he walked east to the Sierra Nevada and Yosemite Valley, a magical-sounding place he'd read about. He fell in love with the mountains, calling them "the range of light." Over the years John studied glaciers, climbed trees, slept outside, and enjoyed more outdoor adventures. He roamed everywhere, filling journals with sketches, pressed plants, and notes.

These little jottings later became nature and travel essays. John sold one essay, then another, recognizing that he might make a living doing "pen work." His powerful words would influence others, including presidents, to preserve open space for future generations.

To learn more, read my biography, *John Muir: Wilderness Protector*, and find other books about or by John Muir. Read *John Muir in His Own Words: A Book of Quotations* and think about how you might relate his quotes to your own life. With paper and pencil, step outside to write about what you see, hear, or even smell. A spider spinning? A coyote howling? Or skunk perfume drifting on the wind?

Start to experience love of anything that is wild.

"A BOY, BLOOMERS, AND BASEBALL IN THE WEST:
SMOKY JOE WOOD AND THE BLOOMER GIRLS" BY JOHNNY D. BOGGS

You won't find Smoky Joe Wood (1889–1985) in the Baseball Hall of Fame in Cooperstown, New York, but in the early 1900s he was one of Major League Baseball's most dominant pitchers. He even pitched the Boston Red Sox to the 1912 World Series championship—winning three games against the New York Giants when he was only twenty-two years old—and spent fourteen years in the big leagues. But Joe never really liked talking about his first experience as a "professional" baseball player. That's because six years before his World Series season, the Kansas schoolboy, then just sixteen, posed as a girl for what was, allegedly, a female team known as the Bloomer Girls. Traveling in a special train across the Midwest, the Bloomer Girls played teams of male players. As one newspaper reported: "Joe has a girlish face, and it was easy for him to pass as a girl."

You can learn more about Joe in *Smoky Joe Wood: The Biography of a Baseball Legend* by Gerald C. Wood, and in *The Glory of Their Times: The Story of the Early Days of Baseball Told by the Men Who Played It* by Lawrence S. Ritter, or visit the Ness County Historical Museum in Wood's hometown, Ness City, Kansas. To learn about the Bloomer Girls, read *Bloomer Girls: Women Baseball Pioneers* by Debra A. Shattuck.

"EARL BASCOM AND HIS BRONC-BUSTIN' BROTHERS:
FATHERS OF MODERN RODEO" BY ROD MILLER

Rodeo is an action-packed sport developed by cowboys and cowgirls. It originated from the everyday jobs cowboys do and grew into competition for the love of it and for the excitement of working (and playing) with horses and cattle.

Over the years, many innovations and improvements made rodeo safer and more exciting. Behind many of those innovations was one cowboy: Earl Bascom. A longtime star of the rodeo circuit through the 1930s, Earl and his brothers gained fame for their abilities and inventions across Canada and the United States. As they traveled the rodeo circuit and put on rodeos of their own, they always looked for ways to do things better, and to make thing safer in the rodeo arena for cowboys and livestock.

As a result, Earl and the Bascom brothers have become known as the "Fathers of Modern Rodeo," along with many other honors and recognition. Today, the Bascom name will be found in rodeo and sports Halls of Fame and museums throughout North America.

You can learn more about rodeo history online at the National Cowboy and Western Heritage Museum and the Professional Rodeo Cowboys Association websites, and about Earl Bascom at BascomBronze.com.

"UNBREAKABLE NAVAJOS" BY JOSEPH BRUCHAC

A group of Navajo Marines, some of the most important heroes of World War II, were neither recognized nor honored until long after the war. These courageous men had been forced to speak only English while in Indian boarding schools. Then, at the request of the United States Marine Corps, they used their once-forbidden Dineh language to create a code for radio transmissions. That Navajo code, which they kept secret for decades, was never broken by the enemy and was used to deliver the most crucial messages across the vast Pacific theater of war. It was not until the 1960s, when computers could do the job of sending messages more efficiently than Navajo code talkers, that their story was made public. I had the good fortune to meet and learn from a number of those Navajo men while I was researching my novel *Code Talker*.

More of their story and the code they created can now be found online at https://navajocodetalkers.org. There are also two recent books in which Navajo code talkers tell their own stories: *Under the Eagle* by Samuel Holiday and Robert S. McPherson, and *Code Talker* by Chester Nez and Judith Avila.

"FIRE AND TRAGEDY: JOE THURSTON AND THE GRANITE MOUNTAIN HOTSHOTS" BY RACHELLE "ROCKY" GIBBONS

On June 30, 2013, an elite group of wildland firefighters known as the Granite Mountain Hotshots responded to a call near the town of Yarnell in central Arizona. They were summoned to do what they did best—establish a "fire line" to starve the fire of the vegetation feeding it. It was expected to be routine duty but turned out to be anything *but*, since the wind direction freakishly turned the fire 180 degrees, cutting off the Hotshots' safety zone and forcing them to deploy survival shelters. By 5:00 p.m. that evening, nineteen crew members were dead, victims of the raging inferno that overtook them. One of those valiant firefighters was my cousin, Joe Thurston, a family man with a loving wife, two young sons, and truly Western roots. This is Joe's story, and the story of the final call of his brave band of brothers, the Granite Mountain Hotshots.

You can read more about them in *The Fire Line* by Fernanda Santos, and in *My Lost Brothers* by Brendan McDonough with Stephan Talty, or visit the Granite Mountain Hotshots Memorial State Park, just west of Yarnell, Arizona.

"HOLIDAYS ON THE FRONTIER" BY SHERRY MONAHAN

Holidays were a big deal for kids on the frontier because they were a time for celebration. They also offered a special chance for young people to see their friends, since many lived in rural areas and were separated from each other by long distances. Families loaded their wagons and headed to town where they ate yummy food, played fun games, and exchanged gifts. "Holidays on the

Frontier" describes how some well-known holidays were observed in the 1800s. It's fun to see how people celebrated back then and compare it with what we do today.

Want more? Check out stories written by kids who lived on the frontier, including those by Ellinor Dale Runcie, Nancy Griswold, and Ella Oblinger. Also check out *Tinsel, Tumbleweeds, and Star-Spangled Celebrations* by Sherry Monahan for even more details about the holidays, and *Frontier Fare*, also by Sherry Monahan, to learn about the food the Western settlers ate.

INDEX

ABOUT THE AUTHORS

LARRY BJORNSON

Spur Award–winning author of the novel *Wide Open*, Larry graduated from the University of California with degrees in history, political science, and public administration. His family owns and operates a North Dakota farm purchased seventy-five years ago by his grandfather (who once played a violin piece for Buffalo Bill Cody).

MATTHEW P. MAYO

Matthew P. Mayo is an award-winning author of novels and short stories. He and his wife, videographer Jennifer Smith-Mayo, along with their trusty pup, Miss Tess, rove the byways of North America in search of hot coffee and high adventure. For more information, drop by Matthew's website at MatthewMayo.com.

JEAN A. LUKESH

Jean A. Lukesh, EdD, is a former teacher and school librarian, a member of Western Writers of America, and a WWA Spur Award recipient and Spur Award finalist for teen nonfiction. She has written five biographies and a Nebraska history textbook, earning fifteen national book awards and Nebraska's Mari Sandoz Award. Her short story about Eagle of Delight was adapted from her book *Eagle of Delight: Portrait of the Plains Indian Girl in the White House*, published by Field Mouse Productions, 2013. The book has received eight national book awards, including the 2014 Western Writers of America Spur Award for Juvenile Nonfiction.

WILLIAM GRONEMAN III

William Groneman III is a former New York City firefighter and a sustaining member of Western Writers of America. He writes about the Alamo, Davy Crockett, John Steinbeck, and the FDNY. He received Western Writers of America's Branding Iron Award in 2019.

EASY JACKSON

Books by Easy Jackson, aka Vicky J. Rose, include the *Tennessee Smith Western* series, *A Bad Place to Die* and *A Season in Hell*, published by Kensington/Pinnacle. Other books include *Muskrat Hill*, a Western mystery published by Five Star, and *Treasure Hunt in Tie Town* and *Testimony*, published by Wolfpack under the name V. J. Rose.

CHRIS ENSS

Chris Enss is a *New York Times* bestselling author who has written more than thirty nonfiction books about women of the Old West.

CANDY MOULTON

Candy Moulton, a two-time Spur Award winner, has pushed and pulled a handcart across the Mormon Pioneer Trail and written a book about the handcart migration, in addition to making a documentary film *In Pursuit of a Dream*, which involved twenty-four young people traveling the trail by wagon train and with handcarts, learning the lessons from the trail. She lives on a ranch near Encampment, Wyoming.

QUACKGRASS SALLY

Quackgrass Sally is a working ranch wife and freelance author in Montana. She writes about the West from her own experiences, having ridden her horse and driven her covered wagon thousands of miles along the Western Historic Trails. She is an active patron member of Western Writers of America and a lifetime member of the National Pony Express Association, as well as one of its first female relay riders. Over the years she has relayed mail and taken part in many events involving the Pony Express (XP), from Washington, DC, to Tasmania. She was also chosen as one of the XP Olympic torch bearers, riding a borrowed horse named Walter near Big Springs, Nebraska. She recounts a funny memory: "Riders had been told the Olympic torch had been tested in wind tunnels and all types of wild weather. Unfortunately, they never tested it in Nebraska's wind, and during the evening relay the torch kept blowing out. I and several other riders ended up carrying the "Mother Lantern," with the flame enclosed in metal and glass. It was heavy and hissed loudly, so I had to keep changing hands while I rode. In that swaying lantern light, I kept seeing Walter's ears twitching every mile of the relay, but he never hesitated and neither did I. We carried out our relay in true XP fashion."

CANDACE SIMAR

Candace Simar is fascinated by how things might have been. Her historical fiction has received awards from the Western Writers of America, the Midwest Book Awards, Women Writing the West, the Western Fictioneers, and the Will Rogers Medallion Awards. Learn more about Candace at www.candacesimar.com.

S. J. DAHLSTROM

S. J. Dahlstrom lives in West Texas with his wife and children. A fifth-generation Texan, Dahlstrom's *Wilder Good* series has won the Wrangler Award from the National Cowboy & Western Heritage Museum, three Will Rogers Medallion Awards, and has been a finalist for the Lamplighter Award and the Spur Award from Western Writers of America.

NANCY OSWALD

Nancy Oswald loves the West and writing about it. Oswald's books have won numerous awards and finalist awards, including the Willa Literary Award and the Western Writers of America Spur Award. She lives with her husband, cows, dogs, cats, and one nearly human donkey on their family ranch in Colorado.

VONN MCKEE

Vonn McKee, Louisiana born and descended from horse traders and southern belles, is a two-time Western Writers of America Spur Award finalist for short fiction. Based in Nashville, she enjoys antiquing, road trips, exploring historic sites, and hiking. Her website is vonnmckee.com.

NANCY PLAIN

A four-time Spur Award winner for her YA nonfiction, Nancy has also received the National Outdoor Book Award, two Nebraska Book Awards, and was named a finalist for the YALSA Excellence in Nonfiction Award. WWA president from 2018 to 2020, Nancy loves the American West for its beauty, its spirit, and its stories. "Solomon D. Butcher, Camera-Toting Pioneer" was adapted from her book *Light on the Prairie: Solomon D. Butcher, Photographer of Nebraska's Pioneer Days*, published by the University of Nebraska Press. Visit www.nancyplain.com.

BILL MARKLEY

Bill Markley has stood at the site of Theodore Roosevelt's Elkhorn Ranch and canoed the Little Missouri River, where TR chased his river pirates. Bill writes nonfiction and historical fiction books, as well as stories and features for Western magazines. His latest book is *Geronimo and Sitting Bull: Indian Leaders of the Legendary West*. A version of his story from this volume, "Tracking Roosevelt's River Pirates," was first published in the June 2011, issue of *True West Magazine*.

GINGER WADSWORTH

Ginger Wadsworth writes nonfiction books for young readers that feature natural science or American heroes. A native Californian, she often writes about her beloved American West. *Camping with the President*, *Yosemite's Songster: One Coyote's Story*, and *Season of the Bear: A Yosemite Story* are Western Writers of America Spur Award winners. Her website is GingerWadsworth.com.

JOHNNY D. BOGGS

Johnny D. Boggs is Western Writers of America's 2020 Owen Wister Award recipient for lifetime achievement. Winner of a record eight Spur Awards, including three for juvenile fiction, Boggs lives in Santa Fe, New Mexico, where he umpires Little League Baseball games in his spare time. His website is JohnnyDBoggs.com.

ROD MILLER

Rod Miller is a four-time winner and six-time finalist for the Western Writers of America Spur Award, recognized for his novels, short stories, poems, and a song. He writes fiction, poetry, and history related to the American West, and his work has been featured in numerous anthologies and magazines.

JOSEPH BRUCHAC

Joseph Bruchac is an enrolled member of the Nulhegan Band of the Coosuk Abenaki Nation. Founder of The Greenfield Review Press, much of his own writing draws on his Native ancestry. Author of more than 160 books for young readers and adults, including his Spur Award–winning novel *Geronimo*, his experiences include three years of volunteer teaching in Ghana, West Africa, and eight years of running a college program in a maximum security prison.

RACHELLE "ROCKY" GIBBONS

Rocky is a two-time Spur Award finalist from the Western Writers of America and currently serves as the WWA membership chair. She grew up along the San Pedro River in southern Arizona and now lives near St. George, Utah.

SHERRY MONAHAN

Sherry is an award-winning author who writes nonfiction books and magazine articles with a historical focus on food, drinks, and daily life. She is a past president of Western Writers of America, and a member of the James Beard Foundation and other organizations. Sherry is also a professional genealogist and an honorary Dodge City marshal.

CPSIA information can be obtained
at www.ICGtesting.com
Printed in the USA
BVHW051311270321
603295BV00002B/5

9 781493 051076